CW01645382

SEPTEMBER

FIRST YEAR

FIRST WEEK

Monday

Show the children a sunflower. What is it? Who can think of another flower of the same color? (Nasturtium, goldenrod, dandelion, buttercup, etc.) Who can think of a flower that is blue? (Hyacinth, bachelor's button, flower de luce, etc.) Who can think of a flower that is red? (Rose, carnation, geranium, poppy, etc.) Have each child name some flower that he likes.

Tuesday

Allow the children to play "Hey, diddle, diddle." One child is the cat, another the fiddle, a third the dish, others the spoon, the little dog, the cow and the moon. All the rest of the children repeat, very slowly:

Hey, diddle, diddle,
The cat and the fiddle.

As the two lines are being recited, the children representing the cat and the fiddle stand up at their seats and bow. As the words,

The cow jumped over the moon,

are recited, the child representing the moon, stooping down, holds out a round piece of pasteboard, a piece of paper, or anything else that happens to be handy, even a book will serve, and the "cow," steps or jumps over it.

At the words,

> The little dog laughed to see such sport,

the little dog laughs. At

> The dish ran away with the spoon,

the two children representing dish and spoon take hold of hands and run across the room.

Then other children may be selected for the various parts, and the game may be played thus again and again.

Wednesday

Have the children practise writing their names, and if possible, their home addresses.

Thursday

What kind of a day is it, sunny or stormy? What color is sunshine? Point to the sun. What color are storm clouds? How does the rain come down? What does the sunshine do for the trees and flowers? What does the rain do for the trees and flowers? What does the rain do for us?

Friday

Have the children name all the objects they can see in the school-room.

SECOND WEEK

Monday

How many children had their faces washed before coming to school this morning? How many had their hair combed? Have each child tell who combed his hair, whether mother, nurse, or the child himself. Talk about the necessity of cleanliness, and why every child must come to school looking clean and tidy.

Tuesday

Write the name of the day of the week on the blackboard, and have the children practice writing it.

Wednesday

Ask each child to stand up at his seat and recite a “Mother Goose” rhyme.

Thursday

Who can show me what I mean when I say, “Run.” Allow some child to run. What do I mean when I say, “Walk.” Have the word illustrated. Continue similarly with *talk*, *laugh*, *sing*, *jump*, *sit*, *stand*.

Friday

Show the children a flag. What is it? What are the three colors of the flag? Have the children count the red stripes; the white stripes. What is the color of the stars?

THIRD WEEK

Monday

Show the children a red apple and a green, or a yellow apple. What are the colors of the two apples? What shape? Where is the stem? Where is the skin? What is there inside the skin? Cut one of the apples open. How many seeds has it?

Tuesday

Have each child tell his father's or his mother's first name.

Wednesday

Have the children practise writing the date.

Thursday

Have each child tell something that he can see out of the school-room window. Write the word given by each child on paper and let him practise writing it.

Friday

Let the children dramatize, with a little suggestive help, "Old King Cole."

FOURTH WEEK

Monday

What day of the week is this? How many days are there in a week? Who can name them? What is done in your home on Monday? (Washing?) On Tuesday? (Ironing?) On Wednesday? Thursday? Friday? Saturday? Sunday?

Tuesday

Have the children play the game, "This is the way we wash our clothes."

Wednesday

Practise writing *September*.

Thursday

Practise writing the day of the week.

Friday

Have the children tell what they had for breakfast.

SECOND YEAR

FIRST WEEK

Monday

Tell, or read, the following story, the children to guess what animal is referred to.

Look what a small, shy thing I am! Do not frighten me, and I will tell you all about myself. It is quite true that I come and nibble your cheese and candles now and then. But if you will keep such nice things stored away in heaps, how can I help longing for a taste? The smell of your puddings and pie-crust is so nice! How should I know that it belongs to you and not to me?

Please do not tell the cat where I am, or she will come and eat me up. I do not like cats a bit. But there is something that I hate more than cats, and that is the horrid traps you set to catch us in. When one of my friends finds himself inside of one of these, you do not know how badly he feels! How would you like it yourself?

We do some good in the world, though people fancy we do nothing but harm. Men and women throw about bits or scraps of food enough to give us many a nice meal. We run out and eat this, and leave the floor clean and tidy.

We run off to our holes as quickly as can be if you frighten us, and you will see no more of our soft fur and long tails. If you are kind we shall be glad to make friends with you.—*Adapted.*

Tuesday

Have the children tell, in their own words, the story of "The Mouse."

Wednesday

Copy the following:

A mouse has gray fur.
A mouse has bright eyes.

Thursday

Have each child tell about some animal, the other children to guess the animal meant. For example:

I have four legs. I have fur. When I am hungry I say, "Miow." When I am happy I purr. What am I?

If you find it to be too difficult for the children to give the descriptions, you can describe the animals, and let all the children guess what you are describing.

Friday

Write five words that rhyme with *cat*.

SECOND WEEK

Monday

What month is this? How many months are there in the year? How many days in this month? Teach the rhyme, "Thirty days hath September."

Tuesday

Have the children write the names of the months.

Wednesday

Have the children complete the following sentences:

Roses are ——.
Asters are ——.
Goldenrod is ——.

Lemons are ——.
Trees are ——.
My eyes are ——.

Thursday

To be memorized:

MY SHADOW

I have a little shadow that goes in and out with me,
And what can be the use of him is more than I can see.
He is very, very like me from the heels up to the head;
And I see him jump before me, when I jump into my bed.

The funniest thing about him is the way he likes to grow—
Not at all like proper children, which is always very slow;
For he sometimes shoots up taller, like an Indian-rubber ball,
And he sometimes gets so little that there's none of him at all.

He hasn't got a notion of how children ought to play,
And can only make a fool of me in every sort of way.
He stays so close beside me, he's a coward you can see;
I'd think shame to stick to nursie as that shadow sticks to me!

One morning, very early, before the sun was up,
I rose and found the shining dew on every buttercup;
But my lazy little shadow, like an arrant sleepy-head,
Had stayed at home behind me and was fast asleep in bed.

—Robert Louis Stevenson.

Have the children copy two stanzas of the poem.

Friday

Have the children copy the rest of the poem, "My Shadow."

THIRD WEEK

Monday

Teach the children the first stanza of "My Shadow."

Who has a shadow? When can we see our shadow? How does the shadow "Jump before me, when I jump into my bed"?

Tuesday

Teach the second stanza of "My Shadow."

How does the shadow grow tall? How does it get "so little"?

Wednesday

Teach the third stanza of "My Shadow," questioning the children to make sure that they understand its meaning.

Thursday

Teach the fourth stanza of "My Shadow."

Friday

Have the children repeat the entire poem, "My Shadow."

FOURTH WEEK

Monday

Write five sentences, telling what the shadow does. (Refer to the poem.)

Tuesday

Write five name words (nouns), to be found in the poem "My Shadow."

Wednesday

Write a letter to your sister or brother, telling what you do at school.

Thursday

Make an envelope of paper, and address it to the one to whom you wrote yesterday.

Friday

Write five words that rhyme with *run*.

To the Teacher: The proper method of addressing an envelope may be taught here.

THIRD YEAR

FIRST WEEK

Monday

Have the children repeat the old rhyme, "Peter Piper picked a peck of pickled peppers," then let them see if they can write it.

Tuesday

For dictation:

I know that when my bed-time comes,
And I am tired of everything,
I cannot go to sleep unless
I hear my mother softly sing
The Bye-low song.

Wednesday

Story for reproduction:

JIM CROW

When Jim Crow became a member of our family he was very young, and could hardly balance himself upon his slender legs.

We fed him upon raw eggs and scraps of raw meat until he grew strong and the black feathers had become smooth and glossy, and the bright eyes were brighter, and Jim Crow had changed into a beautiful bird.

A smart bird was Jim, devoted to his master and mistress, hailing them with a loud caw whenever their steps were heard, and hopping about to greet them.

Jim could talk a little, and would have acquired much more knowledge of the language if he had lived longer.

He would spread his wings, purple in their deep black, and call in a hoarse voice, "Come on, come on," very distinctly.

He would greet his master with "Hello, Papa," and delighted in feeding from his hand. He knew when the butcher boy came with the meat, and was at the cook's side when she received the basket, croaking for his share.

Jim delighted in a plunge bath, and would splash away in an earthern crock a dozen times a day, if it was filled for him.

He liked red and blue, and if ladies called at the house dressed in these colors, the young crow would become frantic, spreading his wings and tail, and crying, "Come on, Come on," to the amusement of all.

He would often eat corn with the chickens, and would act in a very greedy way, filling his bill with the grain, rushing away and hiding it, then coming back for more. If the chickens did not eat as fast as they could, Jim had the lion's share.

Jim was hurt one day by a stray dog, and then we didn't have a crow any more.—*Selected.*

Thursday

Have the children tell, in their own words, the story of "Jim Crow."

Friday

Have the children write the story of "Jim Crow."

SECOND WEEK

Monday

Poem to be memorized:

THE LAND OF STORY BOOKS

At evening when the lamp is lit,
Around the fire my parents sit;
They sit at home, and talk and sing,
And do not play at anything.

Now, with my little gun, I crawl
All in the dark along the wall,
And follow 'round the forest track
Away behind the sofa back.

There, in the night, where none can spy,
All in my hunter's camp I lie
And play at books that I have read
Till it is time to go to bed.

These are the hills, these are the woods,
These are my starry solitudes,
And there the river, by whose brink
The roaring lions come to drink.

I see the others far away,
As if in firelit camp they lay,
And I, like to an Indian scout,
Around their party prowled about.

So when my nurse comes in for me,
Home I return across the sea,
And go to bed with backward looks
At my dear Land of Story Books.
—*Robert Louis Stevenson*

Have the poem copied.

Tuesday

Have the children commit to memory the first two stanzas of "The Land of Story Books."

Wednesday

Have the children commit to memory the third and fourth stanzas of "The Land of Story Books."

Thursday

Have the pupils commit the entire poem, "The Land of Story Books."

Friday

Repeat the poem of the week, entire.

THIRD WEEK

Monday

Write a list of the adjectives to be found in the poem, "The Land of Story Books."

Tuesday

Write a list of the verbs to be found in the poem, "The Land of Story Books."

Wednesday

Write two words that rhyme with each of the following: Sit, wall, bed, lay, sea.

Thursday

Write, in complete sentences, answers to the following questions, referring to the poem for the answers:

What do my parents do?
Where do I go with my gun?
What do I play?
What do I play that I am?
How long do I play?

Friday

Write a letter, thanking your aunt for a birthday present, and telling what the present is.

FOURTH WEEK

Monday

Complete the following sentences:

I am —— to New York.
I —— to school yesterday.
Will you —— to the circus with me?
Has your aunt —— home yet?
Are you —— to school to-morrow?
Shall we —— part way home with you?

Tuesday

Write the names of five objects made of wood; five of iron; five of wool; five of cotton.

Wednesday

Write a composition telling about grapes.

Thursday

Write a letter telling a friend about a squirrel you once saw.

Friday

Write an invitation to a school party.

FOURTH YEAR

FIRST WEEK

Monday

Write five sentences telling about good manners in the school-room.

Tuesday

Describe, orally, some game you know how to play.

Wednesday

Copy the following from Whittier's "The Barefoot Boy":

How the tortoise bears his shell,
How the woodchuck digs his cell,
How the ground-mole sinks his well,
How the robin feeds her young,
How the oriole's nest is hung;
Where the whitest lilies blow,
Where the freshest berries grow,
Where the ground-nut trails its vine,
Where the wood-grape's clusters shine.

Thursday

Write sentences explaining each reference in the poem copied yesterday. For example, "How the tortoise bears his shell"—The tortoise carries his shell on his back.

Friday

Have pupils dramatize "Little Red Riding Hood," without preparation, and in their own way.

SECOND WEEK

Monday

For dictation:

Ere, in the northern gale,
The summer tresses of the leaves are gone,
The woods of Autumn, all around our vale,
Have put their glory on.
—*William Cullen Bryant*

Tuesday

Proverbs, to be copied and committed to memory:

He who does his best, does well.
It takes two to make a quarrel.
Make hay while the sun shines.
More haste, less speed.
Waste not, want not.
A place for everything, and everything in its place.
A friend in need is a friend indeed.
Better late than never.
Look before you leap.
Honesty is the best policy.

Wednesday

Write a composition about “Sparrows.”

Thursday

Write a telegram, congratulating either President Taft or Governor Wilson upon his nomination for President.

Friday

Conversation on how we can tell that Fall and Winter are coming.

THIRD WEEK

Monday

Copy the following from “Hiawatha.”

THE FEAST OF MONDAMIN

And the maize-field grew and ripened,
Till it stood in all the splendor
Of its garments green and yellow,
Of its tassels and its plumage,
And the maize-ears full and shining
Gleamed from bursting sheaths of verdure.

Then Nokomis, the old woman,
Spake and said to Minnehaha:
"Tis the Moon when leaves are falling;
All the wild rice has been gathered,
And the maize is ripe and ready;
Let us gather in the harvest,
Let us wrestle with Mondamin,
Strip him of his plume and tassels,
Of his garments green and yellow."

Tuesday

Commit to memory the selection from "Hiawatha."

Wednesday

Conversation on the meaning of the "Mondamin" story.

Thursday

Write a story on "Corn—How It Grows."

Friday

Write ten sentences about the uses of corn.

FOURTH WEEK

Monday

Write the abbreviations for *month, year*, the days of the week, the months of the year.

Tuesday

For dictation:

Chestnuts in the ashes
  Bursting through the rind,
Red leaf and yellow leaf
  Rustling down the wind;
Mother "doin' peaches"
  All the afternoon—
Don't you think that Autumn's
  Pleasanter than June?

Wednesday

Write five reasons why autumn is pleasanter than June.

Thursday

Write ten sentences containing the word blue.

Friday

Write a rhyme of four lines about apples.

OCTOBER

FIRST YEAR

FIRST WEEK

Monday

What is the name of this month? What was last month called? What month follows October? What season is this? What season follows autumn? What are the four seasons? How do you know that it is autumn? How is the weather different from what it was in July? What are the birds doing this month? What is happening to the leaves on the trees? What flowers are in blossom this month?

Tuesday

A little verse to learn:

Work, and make the world sweet,
That's the best for you.

Wednesday

Read this little poem to the children:

LITTLE MISS CHESTNUT

Little Miss Chestnut lived in a tree,
She and her sisters; one, two, three.
Their house was covered with prickles green,
To keep the squirrels away, I ween.

Soon Jack Frost knocked, just for fun;
Out jumped the chestnuts, every one.

Elsie and Fred, on their walk next day,
Found the nuts and took them away.
On winter evenings, cold and long,
They'll roast the nuts. Here ends my song.

—*Selected*

Have ready, but out of sight, a chestnut burr, if possible containing some of the nuts. If you cannot get the burr, at least have some of the nuts enough so that each child may have one to eat, after the lesson is over.

Show the children how the prickly burr protects the nuts from squirrels, and from boys and girls, until the nuts are ripe. Then Jack Frost comes along and opens the burr, and the nuts fall out.

Explain how the nut itself is the seed of the chestnut tree, and how, if allowed to lie under the snow all winter, a new little chestnut tree will start up in the spring.

Thursday

Teach this little rhyme to the children:

When we have a pleasant day,
We like to stroll along the way;
And as we walk upon the street,
The folks we know we always greet.

Use the rhyme as a means of teaching the children the proper method of salutation on the street. Let the girls wear their hats, and the boys have their caps at their seats with them. Allow a boy and a girl, with hats on, to go to the front of the room, and from opposite sides of the room walk towards each other. As they start, the children—all except the two at the front—repeat the rhyme. When the two children at the front meet, the girl nods her head politely, and the boy lifts his hat. After the simple ceremony the two children return to their seats, and their places are taken by other boys and girls, in turn, until all can perform the act easily and gracefully.

Friday

Ask each child to bring a penny to school. See how many things are to be found on the penny—as a head, date, etc.

SECOND WEEK

Monday

Tell the children that October was the month when America was discovered. We live in the United States, and the United States is in America. Tell the story of Columbus and the discovery of the new continent. If well told, the story is quite as fascinating as a fairy tale.

Tuesday

Have the children tell back to you the story of Columbus and the discovery of America.

Wednesday

A poem dramatized.

This poem, acted out as indicated, can be used effectively as a rest exercise. As all the children will be moving, the windows can be thrown open, and the room aired while the game is being played.

The poem is to be recited by the teacher. Allow plenty of time between lines, for each part to be acted.

Children representing Sunshine, Miss Weather and Professor Wind are first chosen. They take their places in the front of the room. Then the other children are separated, by rows of desks, into Ashes, Oaks, Maples, and Chestnuts.

October gave a party;
The leaves by hundreds came—

The Ashes, Oaks, Maples, and Chestnuts come skipping, tiptoe, up the aisles, helter-skelter, to represent flying leaves.

The Ashes, Oaks, and Maples,
And those of every name.

The skipping is continued, until all the leaves stand in a group at one side of the room.

Miss Sunshine spread a carpet,
And everything was grand.

As these two lines are being recited Miss Sunshine pretends to spread a carpet over the entire open space at the front of the room. She may take plenty of time. The poem is not to be recited continuously.

Miss Weather led the dancing,

As this line is recited, Miss Weather skips alone across the front of the room, from one side to the other.

Professor Wind, the band.

Professor Wind marches pompously across the room, tooting a real or an imaginary horn.

The Chestnuts came in yellow,

The Chestnuts skip lightly, by couples, from one side of the room to the side where Miss Weather stands. They bow to Miss Weather by twos, turn, and skip back again.

The Oaks in crimson dressed;
The lovely Misses Maple
In scarlet looked their best.

The Oaks, then the Maples, followed by the Ashes, skip across the room by twos, bowing to Miss Weather, and returning to their places, after the fashion of the Chestnuts.

And balanced all their partners,
And gaily fluttered by;
The sight was like a rainbow
Now fallen from the sky.

While the teacher is reciting the four lines given above, all the children are still, but at its close, all skip about partners, holding their clasped hands high above the head, skipping tiptoe, as before, and very light and gay.

Then in the rustic hollows,
   At "hide-and-seek" they played,
The party closed at sundown,
   And everybody stayed.

All remain quiet while the four lines given above are recited, then partners separate, and everybody apparently hides somewhere.

Professor Wind played louder;
   They flew along the ground;
And then the party ended
   In jolly hands around.

As Professor Wind blows his hardest, all gather from their hiding places, take hold of hands and circle round, and the game ends.

—Selected and adapted

Thursday

Play the October game.

Friday

Play the October game.

THIRD WEEK

Monday

Read this poem to the children, for them to guess who is meant:

WHO'S THE ROGUE?

A roguish old fellow is prowling about
In field and in garden; you can't keep him out.
No matter how tall
You build up your wall,
He'll find a way over, in spite of it all.

On the glass of the window his pictures you'll see,
A grand exhibition (admission is free);
He works hard at night
While the stars glitter bright;
But when the sun rises he keeps out of sight.

He'll sketch you a snow-covered mountain or tree;
A torrent all frozen, a ship out at sea.
He draws very fast,
But his work does not last:
It fades when the chill of the night-time is past.

Before the sun rises, while hardly 'tis light,
He feels of the fruit and takes a sly bite;
He has a fine taste,
Though a great deal he'll waste,
Then off he will go in very great haste.

Now, who do you think this old fellow may be,
The bright, sparkling work of whose fingers we see?
All winter he'll stay,
What more shall I say?
Only this, that his first name begins with a J.

—Selected

Tuesday

On this, or some rainy morning of the week, talk about the weather. Why did you all come to school this morning with rubbers and umbrellas? Why is an umbrella shaped as it is? Why does the rain sometimes fall straight down, and sometimes slanting? How does the rain tell us which way the wind blows? Why do rubbers keep our feet dry, when shoes do not? What else is made of rubber?

Wednesday

Teach the children this memory gem:

All that's great and good is done
Just by patient trying.

Thursday

What does Jack Frost do to the windows? What does he do to the nuts? What does he do to the apples? What does he do to the grass? What are some other things that Jack Frost does?

Friday

Play the October game, described under the preceding week.

FOURTH WEEK

Monday

An October Pumpkin Story. (To be told to the children.)

One afternoon in late October, father went down to the field to get a pumpkin.

The children went along too. They wanted to see that father picked out a large pumpkin. They wanted to help bring it back to the house.

Although it was October, there were still some pumpkins to be found in the field.

Father led the way. The children came trooping after.

The pumpkins grew down in the cornfield. Their long, coarse stems lay sprawling on the ground. Their big, rough leaves looked like green umbrellas.

The boys saw a very large pumpkin. They were just going to pick it, but father said, "Not that one."

Father looked around until he found a deep, yellow pumpkin. He told the children that deep, yellow pumpkins make the best pies.

The children soon found another pumpkin, somewhat smoother than the others. They picked that to use for a Jack-o'-lantern.

Then they went back to the house, carrying the huge yellow fruit with them.

The girls went into the house, to see mother make pumpkin pies.

Mother cut open the yellow pumpkin. Oh, how thick the meat was! Oh, how the fat, white seeds came tumbling out! Mother said the flesh was good because it had a nice fine grain.

Mother cut the flesh into small pieces, after she had peeled off the thick rind.

Then she put the pieces into a large iron pot to boil.

When the girls had seen the pieces disappear into the pot they went to see what the boys were doing.

Out by the barn they found the boys with a jack-knife, working away at the other pumpkin. The boys were making a Jack-o'-lantern.

They had cut a round hole in the top of the pumpkin, so as to leave the stem for a handle. In this way they could lift out the round piece like a cover. They dug out all the seeds with their hands, to make it hollow.

Then they cut a small hole, shaped like a triangle, in the side of the pumpkin. They bored two round holes, one each side of the triangle. Below it they cut a funny hole shaped like a new moon.

It looked like a huge grinning face. When the boys had finished it, they put the pumpkin away in the barn.

Then they all remembered about the pumpkin that was cooking in the kitchen, so they ran back to the house as fast as they could.

By this time the pumpkin in the pot was done, and mother took it from the stove. She poured off the water, and then put the cooked pumpkin into a colander.

While mother was rubbing the soft pumpkin through the colander, the boys ran off to hunt for eggs. When they came back, mother took eight of the eggs, and about three pints of the soft pumpkin. She stirred it very fast, while the children stood around and watched, with open eyes and mouths. Then she put in milk, and spice, and brown sugar.

Oh, didn't it look good! The children smacked their lips as each separate thing went in. Mother gave it all such a beating with her big spoon that the children said it would be good ever after.

Next came the pie tins lined with soft crust, and last of all the pies went into the oven.

That night as father and mother sat in front of the fire-place talking, a strange noise was heard. What could it be? Was it a groan? Was somebody hurt? There it was again, again, and again! It came from the front porch.

Father went to the window and drew aside the curtain. Then they saw something that made the smaller children shiver, but the older girls only laughed. The boys were not in the house.

There at the window, staring in and grinning horribly—was—well, what do you suppose? Yes it was the Jack-o'-lantern.

—*Selected*

Tuesday

Talk about Jack-o'-lanterns. If possible, make one in school, or show the children one.

Wednesday

Talk about Hallowe'en, and how the Jack-o'-lantern is used for decoration at that time.

Thursday

Talk about Hallowe'en tricks.

Friday

Play some of the Hallowe'en tricks in school.

SECOND YEAR

FIRST WEEK

Monday

To be copied and memorized by the pupils:

THE WORLD'S MUSIC

The world's a very happy place,
Where every child should dance and sing,
And always have a smiling face,
And never sulk for anything.

The world is such a happy place,
That children, whether big or small,
Should always have a shining face,
And never, never sulk at all.

—*Selected*

Tuesday

Have the children write answers, as complete sentences, to the following questions about "The World's Music":

What kind of place is the world?
What should every child have?
What should a child do?
What should a child never do?

Wednesday

Bring sufficient hickory nuts to the class so that each child can have one. If possible, have the nuts in the hulls. Ask the following questions, for the children to answer:

How many hulls on each nut?
What are the hulls for? (To protect the nut.)
What takes off the hulls when they are quite ripe? (The frost.)
Which is the blossom end of the nut, and which is the stem end?
Crack a hickory nut. What is there inside the shell?
Explain how the nut grows, to start a new tree.

Thursday

Copy these sentences, filling the blank spaces with *is*, or *are*:

A gray squirrel —— in the tree.
The squirrel —— fond of nuts.
The tree —— once the squirrel's home.
Hickory nuts —— the squirrel's food.

Friday

For dictation:

I am round.
I am red.
I am just a bit sour.
Would you like to eat me?

SECOND WEEK

Monday

Poem to be memorized.

Commit the first stanza of the poem to memory:

THE WONDERFUL WORLD

Great, wide, wonderful, beautiful world,
With the wonderful water around you curled,
And the wonderful grass upon your breast—
World, you are beautifully dressed!

The wonderful air is over me,
And the wonderful wind is shaking the tree;
It walks on the water and whirls the mills,
And talks to itself on the tops of the hills.

You friendly Earth, how far do you go,
With wheat fields that nod, and rivers that flow,
With cities and gardens, and oceans and isles,
And people upon you for thousands of miles?

Ah, you are so great and I am so small,
I hardly can think of you, World, at all;
And yet, when I said my prayers to-day,
My mother kissed me, and said, quite gay:

"If the wonderful World is great to you,
And great to father and mother, too,
You are more than the Earth, though you are such a dot,
You can love and think, and the Earth cannot!"

—*William Brighty Rands*

Tuesday

Commit to memory the second stanza of the poem.

Wednesday

Commit to memory the third stanza of the poem.

Thursday

Commit to memory the fourth stanza of the poem.

Friday

Finish learning the poem, and recite it all.

THIRD WEEK

Monday

The Post-Office.—What is a post-office? Who has charge of the post-office? Where is the post-office nearest your home? What do you see when you go to the post-office? How do you get your mail? Why do people write letters? How do letters go from one place to another? What is the stamp on a letter for? How much does it cost to send a letter? Who pays for sending a letter?

Tuesday

For dictation:

> It is cold in the fall.
> The wind blows hard.
> The trees are bare.
> The birds are gone.
> I like fall, for I can play out-of-doors.

Wednesday

Write a letter to a friend, telling what Jack Frost does in the fall. Send the letter to your friend, directing the envelope properly, and putting the stamp in the right place.

Thursday

Bring to the class cards, each having on it the name of some animal, as cow, horse, elephant, dog, etc. Give a card to each pupil, and have him describe the animal named on his card, allowing the other children to guess what animal he is describing. For example: "I am not very large. I have a bushy tail. I live among the trees. I like to eat nuts. What am I?"

Friday

For dictation:

One day as Mr. Squirrel went up his tree to bed,
A very large hickory nut fell on his head.
"Although I am fond of nuts," Mr. Squirrel then did say,
"I would very much rather they did not come that way."

FOURTH WEEK

Monday

Tell this story to the children:

JACK FROST AND THE NUTS

Little Miss Chestnut and her two sisters lived up in a tree in a prickly green house. The house was as soft as velvet inside, but sharp spikes on the outside kept away the squirrels, who would have torn down the house if they could.

But soon Jack Frost came along. Jack does not mind fences, so he knocked at the door of the Chestnut house.

"Little Miss Chestnut," he called, "are you ready to come out?"

But little Miss Chestnut replied, "I am not quite ready yet, Mr. Jack."

So Jack went off to the house where Miss Hickory Nut lived. Miss Hickory Nut lived all alone in a round green cottage.

"Miss Hickory Nut," he called "are you ready to come out?"

But Miss Hickory Nut replied, "I am not quite ready yet, Mr. Jack."

So Jack went off to the low bush where Miss Hazel Nut lived in a soft green tent. Miss Hazel Nut was already peeping out.

"Miss Hazel Nut," he called, "are you ready to come out?"

And little Miss Hazel Nut replied, "I am quite ready, Mr. Jack."

So she dropped down and waited below the bush, while Jack went back after the other nuts.

Jack knocked once more at the chestnut house. Little Miss Chestnut opened the door so quickly that she and her sisters fell to the ground.

Then Jack knocked once more at the hickory house.

Miss Hickory Nut opened the door so quickly that her house fell apart.

And all the other nut houses opened, and all the nuts came out to see what was the matter.

The next day the children went for a walk. As they walked in the woods they spied the nuts.

"See," they said, "the frost has opened the chestnut burrs, and all the other nuts must be out of the shucks."

Tuesday

Have the children tell back to you the story of Jack Frost and the nuts.

Wednesday

Write five sentences about nuts.

Thursday

Write answers to the following questions:

What does Jack Frost do?
Where does he paint pictures? (On the window-pane.)
What colors does he paint the maple leaves?
What colors does he paint the hickory leaves?

Friday

Talk with the children about the way seeds are scattered. Bring to school various kinds of seeds, if these are available. How are dandelion seeds scattered? How are milkweed seeds scattered? How are burdock seeds scattered?

THIRD YEAR

FIRST WEEK

Monday

Read to the children the following poem:

MRS. RED SQUIRREL

Mrs. Red Squirrel sat on the top of a tree;
"I believe in the habit of saving," said she;
"If it were not for that, in the cold winter weather
I should starve, and my young ones, I know, altogether;
But I am teaching my children to run and lay up
Every acorn as soon as it drops from its cup,
And to get out the corn from the shocks in the field—
There's a nice hollow tree where I keep it concealed.

"We have laid up some wheat, and some barley and rye,
And some very nice pumpkin seeds I have put by;
Best of all, we have gathered in all that we could
Of beechnuts and butternuts grown in the wood;
For cold days and hard times winter surely will bring,
And a habit of saving's an excellent thing.

"But my children—you know how young squirrels like play,
'We have plenty, great plenty, already,' they say;
'We are tired of bringing in food for our store;
Let us all have a frolic, and gather no more!'
But I tell them it's pleasant when winter is rough,
If we feel both to use and to give we've enough;
And they'll find, ere the butternuts bloom in the spring,
That a habit of saving's an excellent thing."

—*Selected*

Tuesday

Have the pupils tell back to you, the story of "Mrs. Red Squirrel."

Wednesday

Write five sentences about Mrs. Red Squirrel, and the habit of saving.

Thursday

For dictation:

I am small and nearly round. I have a hard, brown shell. Inside, my meat is brown, too. You like to eat me with a little salt. You get my meat by breaking my shell. What am I?

Friday

Write a story similar to the one given in the lesson for yesterday, for the other pupils to guess. You can write about an apple or some other fruit; about a dog or some other animal; or about a flower.

SECOND WEEK

Monday

Have the children copy the following:

HIAWATHA'S CHILDHOOD

At the door on summer evenings
Sat the little Hiawatha;
Heard the whispering of the pine trees,
Heard the lapping of the water,
Sounds of music, words of wonder;
"Minne-wawa!" said the pine trees,
"Mudway-aushka!" said the water.
Saw the firefly, Wah-wah-taysee,
Flitting through the dusk of evening,
With the twinkle of its candle
Lighting up the brakes and bushes,
And he sang the song of children,
Sang the song Nokomis taught him:
"Wah-wah-taysee, little firefly,
Little, flitting, white-fire insect,
Little, dancing, white-fire creature,
Light me with your little candle,
Ere upon my bed I lay me,
Ere in sleep I close my eyelids!"

Tuesday

Have the children copy the following:

Forth into the forest straightway
All alone walked Hiawatha
Proudly, with his bow and arrows;
And the birds sang round him, o'er him,
"Do not shoot us, Hiawatha!"
Sang the robin, the Opechee,
Sang the bluebird, the Owaissa,
"Do not shoot us, Hiawatha!"
Up the oak tree, close beside him,
Sprang the squirrel, Adjidaumo,
In and out among the branches,
Coughed and chattered from the oak tree,
Laughed, and said between his laughing,
"Do not shoot me, Hiawatha!"

Wednesday

Tell the children the story of Hiawatha. If possible, read the whole part of the poem relating to Hiawatha's childhood. Have the children read the portion of the poem quoted here.

Thursday

What sounds did Hiawatha like to hear on summer evenings? What did he think the pine tree said? The water? What did he call the firefly? What is the firefly's candle? Who taught Hiawatha the song about the firefly?

What did Hiawatha learn from the birds? Who taught him their names? How did he discover their secrets? What secrets are mentioned? What did he call the birds?

Friday

What did Hiawatha call the firefly? Why did he call the firefly, "Little, dancing, white-fire creature"?

What is the difference between "brakes" and "bushes"?

What did Hiawatha call the robin? The bluebird? The squirrel?

What words show the sound of the pine tree? The sound of the water? The motion of the firefly? The sound made by the squirrel?

Tell how Hiawatha spent his evenings.

Describe the little hunter as he went into the forest.

THIRD WEEK

Monday

Write five sentences about the things that Hiawatha heard at the door on summer evenings?

Tuesday

Write five sentences about what happened when Hiawatha went into the forest.

Wednesday

Write what Hiawatha learned of the birds.

Thursday

Write about what Hiawatha learned of the animals.

Friday

Let the children play Hiawatha.

FOURTH WEEK

Spend this entire week on the poem Hiawatha. Let the children dramatize it in their own way, but under your guidance. Let those who have Indian costumes wear them to school. Talk Hiawatha and live Hiawatha, for the entire week. Use the language of the poem yourself, and encourage the children to do so.

FOURTH YEAR

FIRST WEEK

Monday

Poem to be committed to memory:

THE VILLAGE BLACKSMITH

Under a spreading chestnut tree,
  The village smithy stands;
The smith, a mighty man is he,
  With large and sinewy hands;
And the muscles of his brawny arms
  Are strong as iron bands.

His hair is crisp, and black, and long,
  His face is like the tan;
His brow is wet with honest sweat,
  He earns whate'er he can,
And looks the whole world in the face,
  For he owes not any man.

Week in, week out, from morn till night,
  You can hear his bellows blow;
You can hear him swing his heavy sledge,
  With measured beat and slow,
Like a sexton ringing the village bell,
  When the evening sun is low.

The children coming home from school
   Look in at the open door;
They love to see the flaming forge,
   And hear the bellows roar,
And catch the burning sparks that fly
   Like chaff from a threshing floor.

He goes on Sunday to the church,
   And sits among his boys;
He hears the parson pray and preach,
   He hears his daughter's voice,
Singing in the village choir,
   And it makes his heart rejoice.

It sounds to him like her mother's voice,
   Singing in Paradise!
He needs must think of her once more,
   How in the grave she lies;
And with his hard, rough hand he wipes
   A tear out of his eyes.

Toiling—rejoicing—sorrowing,
   Onward through life he goes;
Each morning sees some task begun,
   Each evening sees it close;
Something attempted, something done,
   Has earned a night's repose.

Thanks, thanks to thee, my worthy friend,
   For the lesson thou hast taught!
Thus at the flaming forge of life
   Our fortunes must be wrought;
Thus on its sounding anvil shaped
   Each burning deed and thought!

—Henry Wadsworth Longfellow

Have the entire poem copied.

Spend the rest of the week in having the poem committed to memory.

SECOND WEEK

Monday

Write answers to the following:

Where does the village smithy stand?

Describe the smith.

Write another word whose meaning is similar to "bravery."

What is meant by "crisp" hair?

Why should the smith's face be brown, as though tanned?

Why is sweat called "honest"?

By doing what kinds of work does a smith earn his living?

Why should the smith be able to look the whole world in the face because he owes no one anything?

Has the world a face? What, then, is meant by "looking the whole world in the face"?

Tuesday

Describe the bellows used by the blacksmith.

What is the sledge used by the blacksmith?

Why is the sledge made heavy? Why is it swung slowly?

What is meant by "measured" beat? What is a musical measure?

What is a sexton? Where was the village bell hung, then? Why was it called the "village" bell?

When is the evening sun low?

What is a "forge"?

Why do bellows "roar"?

What is "chaff"? What is a threshing floor? How is grain threshed now-a-days? How was it usually threshed when this poem was written?

Wednesday

What members of the smith's family are mentioned in the poem? What is a parson?

What is a "choir"?

Write a word whose meaning is similar to that of "rejoice."

Why is the smith's hand "hard and rough"?

Write a list of the adjectives used in the poem which are used to describe the smith.

Thursday

Write a word that might have been used in place of "toiling." Which is the more poetic word?

What is a "task"?

What is meant by a "night's repose"? Write another word meaning repose.

Why does something done earn repose?

What is the lesson which the smith teaches?

Friday

Write ten sentences, describing the smith.

THIRD WEEK

Monday

Conversation on signs of the coming of winter.

Tuesday

For dictation:

You cannot change yesterday, that is clear,
Or begin tomorrow until it is here.
So the only thing left, for you and for me,
Is to make to-day as sweet as can be.

Wednesday

Have pupils write about Columbus and the discovery of America.

Thursday

Write an invitation to Hallowe'en exercises to be held at the school.

Friday

Write an answer to the invitation written the day before, accepting the invitation.

FOURTH WEEK

Monday

Write ten sentences containing the word *red*.

Tuesday

Write five sentences, each sentence to end with a word rhyming with *hat*.

Wednesday

Write a description of some Hallowe'en trick.

Thursday

Play the game of "Who am I?" Each pupil play he is some object in the room. He must describe himself so that the rest can guess his name. Each pupil begins his description: "I am not myself. See if you can guess my name." Then follows the description. The pupil who first guesses the object from the description, describes himself next.

Friday

Have a spelling match.

NOVEMBER

FIRST YEAR

FIRST WEEK

Monday

How many days has November? How many days had October? What month comes after November? What day in November do we celebrate? Why do we celebrate Thanksgiving? How do we celebrate Thanksgiving? What kind of weather do we have in November? What season is this? What season follows autumn?

Tuesday

For the children to learn by heart:

To have willing feet,
A smile that is sweet,
A kind, pleasant word
For all that you meet—
That's what it is to be helpful.

Wednesday

Tell the children about the Pilgrims: How they became dissatisfied with conditions in England, because they were not allowed to worship as they wished; their going to Holland, and finally their coming to New England, in the *Mayflower*. Tell about the landing at Plymouth; about little Peregrine White. If possible, show some of the Boughton pictures of life in Plymouth.

Thursday

Tell the children how there was suffering among the Pilgrims, and their fear that they might starve. Tell, with all possible vividness, about the coming of the welcome ship from England; and then, the appointment of a day of Thanksgiving.

Friday

Tell the children what the people had to eat on that first Thanksgiving Day. Tell the story of the corn, and how the Indians had supplied the seed and taught the Pilgrims how to raise it. Where did they get their turkey for the dinner? Why do we like to have turkey for Thanksgiving dinner?

SECOND WEEK

Monday

Teach the children the first three stanzas of the great Thanksgiving poem:

THANKSGIVING DAY

Over the river and through the wood,
To grandfather's house we'll go.
    The horse knows the way
    To carry the sleigh
Through the white and drifted snow.

Over the river and through the wood,
To have a first-rate play,
    Hear the bells ring,
    "Ting-a-ling-ding!"
Hurrah for Thanksgiving Day!

Over the river and through the wood,
Now grandmother's cap I spy!
    Hurrah for the fun!
    Is the pudding done?
Hurrah for the pumpkin pie!
—*Lydia Maria Child*

On Monday recite the poem yourself, allowing the children to say, "Over the river and through the wood," as each stanza is recited. You can recite the poem half a dozen times in this way, and the children will enjoy their part as well as yours.

Tuesday

Teach the children the last line of each of the three stanzas of the poem.

Wednesday

Teach the children the whole of the first stanza of the poem.

Thursday

Teach the children the second stanza of the poem.

Friday

Teach the children all three stanzas of the poem.

THIRD WEEK

Monday

Spend this whole week playing Pilgrim life in old New England. Have the children land from the *Mayflower* on the Plymouth Rock. A desk or chair, or a box will serve for the rock. The passengers will wear their hats, and books will serve as luggage.

Tuesday

Play Pilgrim Sunday. The children can march towards church two by two, with sticks or wands for guns. Tell about the old churches, with their square pews, high pulpits, and sounding board. Explain the duties of the tithing man. If possible, show pictures to illustrate the church scenes.

Wednesday

Play the daily life of the Pilgrims. Pretend to spin, explaining the process; weave, make candles, pound corn to make Indian meal, cook over the fireplace, etc.

Thursday

Things we have to be thankful for: Let the children suggest.

Friday

The Thanksgiving dinner. The turkey. Talk about how it is raised, what it looks like, how it is cooked.

FOURTH WEEK

Monday

The vegetables on the Thanksgiving table. The bread. The fruit. The nuts.

Tuesday

Here is a simple version of the Thanksgiving story, to tell to the children, in its proper place in connection with the lessons of the month.

THE THANKSGIVING STORY

Once upon a time, some of the people of England were in great trouble. The king would not allow them to worship God in the way they thought right.

When they said they must do what they thought right, some of them were whipped, and some of them were put in prison.

At last they decided to leave England, and go to some other country. And they did go, in a ship, to a land where everybody dressed so differently, and spoke such a different language that the English boys and girls could not at first understand them. Holland was the name of the country. How many of you have seen pictures of the Dutch children, who live in Holland? How many of you have seen pictures of Dutch windmills?

Now in Holland, in the course of time, the Dutch and the English children became very good friends. Before very long the English boys and girls were talking Dutch as easily as if they had been born in Holland, and had never heard of any other country.

"My, my," said good Father Brewster, the leader of the Puritans, as they were called. "This will never do. We want our children to talk English, and to love England and her ways"—for the Puritans still loved their country and their flag, just as we love our beautiful flag with the stars and stripes.

"They say," said Father Brewster, "that far away over the ocean there is a land called America. Let us go to America. There we can build houses like those we had in England, and there our children can be brought up as English people. Yes, we will go to America."

So the Puritans engaged two big ships, and started to sail from Holland to America. But one of the ships was too old and too worn out to cross the ocean, so all the people embarked on the other ship and sailed away.

The ship was called the *Mayflower*.

The *Mayflower* was crowded, and it rocked so that the boys and girls became very tired. They wished they could get off and play on land once more.

But two beautiful presents came to interest and amuse them on the long voyage. And what do you think they were? Two little babies. One of them was named Peregrine White. The other was named Oceanus Hopkins, because he was born on the ocean.

One morning the children looked far away across the water, and they could see a dark line. It was the land—*America*.

The next day the sails of the ship were taken down, and the anchor was dropped in a little bay. Then some of the men climbed down from the ship into a small boat, and rowed to the shore to see what the place was like. In a little while they came back and called out, "Come, we will take you all ashore."

Such a scurrying and hurrying as there was then! Back and forth the little boat went, until all the boys and girls, and men and women were on the shore.

It was a very cold day, the twenty-second of December, 1620. But they did not mind the cold.

In a little time the men had built some log houses, and soon there was a church. The black rock on which the Pilgrims first stepped can be seen to-day. It is called Plymouth Rock. The first girl to step upon Plymouth rock was Mary Chilton.

One day a visitor came to see the Pilgrims. He was an Indian. He had long, black hair. He was dressed in deerskin. He had a bow and arrows, to shoot birds and deer with.

The Indian was very glad to see the white people. “Welcome, Englishmen,” he said. He stayed over night with the Pilgrims, and the next morning went away.

Soon he came back, bringing some friends with him.

When spring came, the Indians showed the Pilgrims how to catch eels, and where to find fish. They also gave the Pilgrims corn to plant. They showed them how to plant the corn, putting a fish in each hill to make the corn grow well.

All summer long the boys and girls played around the log-houses, and were very happy. There were beautiful wild-flowers, and bright-colored song-birds in the woods where they played. One flower that blossomed in the early spring they named the Mayflower, for the ship in which they had come. The trailing arbutus has been called the Mayflower to this day.

When the summer was ended, and all the corn and wheat were gathered in, the Pilgrims said, “Let us have Thanksgiving Day. We will thank God because he made the sun to shine, and the rain to fall, and the corn to grow.”

Then the mothers said, “We will have a Thanksgiving party, and invite the Indians. We will cook some of everything raised on the farms.”

The men shot deer, and wild geese, and wild turkeys for the dinner, and that is why we like to have roast goose or turkey for our Thanksgiving dinner.

At last the Thanksgiving Day came. In the morning everybody went to church. When they got home they found that all the Indians who had been invited had come.

The Indians brought five large deer. The party lasted for three days. At each meal, before they began to eat, the Pilgrims and the Indians thanked God.

In the evening the Indians sang and danced, and in the daytime they played games with the children.

At last the party was over. When the Indians were going home the Pilgrims said, “Every year we shall have a time to thank God for all He has done for us. You must come and help us thank Him.”

So every year the Pilgrims had their Thanksgiving Day. When other people came to this country they said they would have Thanksgiving too. So for nearly three hundred years we have had the glad Thanksgiving Day. In what month does it come? On what day of November does it come this year?

—Selected

Wednesday

A little prayer to be learned this month:

May we be thankful for the night,
And for the pleasant morning light,
For rest, and food, and loving care,
And all that makes the world so fair.

May we do the things we should;
May we be always kind and good,
In all we do, in work or play,
To grow more loving every day.—*Selected*

Thursday

Talk about signs of winter.

Friday

For the children to learn:

Kind hearts are the gardens,
Kind thoughts are the roots;
Kind words are the flowers,
Kind deeds are the fruits.

SECOND YEAR

FIRST WEEK

Monday

For dictation:

Do all the good you can,
To all you can,
In all the ways you can.

Tuesday

Talk about the way to set a table. What is put on the table first? Where do we place the knives? Where do we place the forks? Where do we place the spoons? Where do we place the glasses? Who serves the meat? Who serves the vegetables? Where are the meat and vegetables placed? Who serves the dessert? Who serves the tea or coffee?

Wednesday

Fable for reproduction: The Fox and the Grapes. One day a hungry fox started out to find something to eat. He saw some grapes, near the top of a tall grapevine.

The fox tried to jump up and get the grapes but he could not reach them. He tried again and again, but it was of no use.

As he walked away, he said, "I do not care for the grapes. They are sour."

Thursday

Have the children dramatize "The Fox and the Grapes." Hang a bunch of grapes over the door or let the children pretend that the grapes are hung there. Have the child who is to play the part of the fox walk along and look up eagerly at the bunch of grapes.

"What beautiful grapes!" he says. "I wish I had some."

Then he jumps and tries to reach them. He tries a second time, and a third. The last time he loses his balance and falls to the floor. He gets up, rubs his head, and says, "I do not care for the grapes. They are sour."

Friday

Write five sentences about the fox and the grapes.

SECOND WEEK

Monday

Read the following poem to the children:

APPLE-SEED JOHN

Poor Johnny was bent well-nigh double
With years of toil and care and trouble;
But his large old heart still felt the need
Of doing for others some kindly deed.

"But what can I do?" old Johnny said;
"I who work so hard for daily bread?
It takes heaps of money to do much good;
I am far too poor to do as I would."

The old man sat thinking deeply awhile,
When over his features gleamed a smile,
And he clapped his hands with boyish glee,
And said to himself, "There's a way for me!"

He worked and he worked with might and main,
But no one knew the plan in his brain
He took ripe apples in pay for chores,
And carefully cut from them all the cores.

He filled a bag full, then wandered away,
And no man saw him for many a day.
With knapsack over his shoulder slung,
He marched along, and whistled or sung.

He seemed to roam with no object in view,
Like one who had nothing on earth to do;
But, journeying thus o'er the prairies wide,

He paused now and then, and his bag untied.

With pointed cane deep holes he would bore,
And in every hole he placed a core;
Then covered them well, and left them there
In keeping of sunshine, rain and air.

Sometimes for days he waded through grass,
And saw not a living creature pass,
But often, when sinking to sleep in the dark,
He heard the owls hoot, and the prairie dogs bark.

Sometimes an Indian of sturdy limb
Came striding along and walked with him;
And he who had food shared with the other,
As if he had met a hungry brother.

When the Indian saw how the bag was filled,
And looked at the holes that the white man drilled,
He thought to himself 'twas a silly plan
To be planting seed for some future man.

Sometimes a log cabin came in view,
Where Johnny was sure to find jobs to do,
By which he gained stores of bread and meat,
And welcome rest for his weary feet.

He had full many a story to tell,
And goodly hymns that he sang right well;
He tossed up the babes, and joined the boys
In many a game full of fun and noise.

And he seemed so hearty, in work or play,
Men, women and boys all urged him to stay;
But he always said, "I have something to do,
And I must go on to carry it through."

The boys, who were sure to follow him round,
Soon found what it was he put in the ground;

And so as time passed and he traveled on,
Ev'ry one called him "Old Apple-seed John."

Whenever he'd used the whole of his store,
He went into cities and worked for more;
Then he marched back to the wilds again,
And planted seed on hillside and plain.

In cities, some said the old man was crazy;
While others said he was only lazy;
But he took no notice of gibes and jeers,
He knew he was working for future years.

He knew that trees would soon abound
Where once a tree could not have been found;
That a flick'ring play of light and shade
Would dance and glimmer along the glade;

That blossoming sprays would form fair bowers,
And sprinkle the grass with rosy showers;
And the little seeds his hands had spread
Would become ripe apples when he was dead.

So he kept on traveling far and wide,
Till his old limbs failed him and he died.
He said at the last, "Tis a comfort to feel
I've done good in the world, though not a great deal."

Weary travelers, journeying west,
In the shade of his trees find pleasant rest;
And they often start, with glad surprise,
At the rosy fruit that round them lies.

And if they inquire whence came such trees,
Where not a bough once swayed in the breeze,
The answer still comes, as they travel on,
"These trees were planted by Apple-seed John."

—*Lydia Maria Child, in St. Nicholas*

Tuesday

Have the children tell back to you the story of Apple-seed John. Ask the following questions, or similar questions. What did Apple-seed John look like? Was he old or young? What did he wish that he might do for people? How did he get his apple cores? How did he carry his apple cores? How did he plant the cores? What did he do when his bag was empty? Why was he called "Old Apple-seed John"? What happened to the cores that he planted? What kind of trees grew from the apple seeds? Who could eat the apples? Do you think his plan of planting apple-trees, a nice one?

Wednesday

Write five sentences about Apple-seed John.

Thursday

Write a letter to a friend, telling about Apple-seed John.

Friday

Play Apple-seed John.

THIRD WEEK

Monday

Have the children copy the following:

LITTLE MISS MUFFET

Little Miss Muffet sat on a tuffet,
Eating of curds and whey;
There came a big spider, and sat down beside her,
And frightened Miss Muffet away.

Tuesday

Allow the pupils to dramatize Little Miss Muffet:

Have a little girl sit on a dry-goods box, holding either a real or a play bowl and spoon. She pretends to eat from the bowl. Have a boy place quietly beside her one of the very realistic Japanese spiders. Suddenly she sees it. She jumps up and runs away. Meanwhile the other children recite the ryhme.

Wednesday

Have the children copy:

Blow, wind, blow!
And go, mill, go!
That the miller may grind his corn;
That the baker may take it,
And into rolls make it,
And send us some hot in the morn.

Thursday

Write a word that describes: *wind, mill, miller, corn, baker, rolls.*

Friday

Write answers to the following, in complete sentences:

What does the wind do?
What does the wind do to the mill?
What does the miller do to the corn?
What does the baker do to the meal?
What becomes of the rolls?

FOURTH WEEK

Monday

Have the children tell, orally, the Thanksgiving story.

Tuesday

Talk about *the chicken*: Where does the chicken come from? What is the color of little chickens? What are the colors of hens? How do a chicken's feathers change as the chicken grows? How many feet has a hen? How many eyes? What kind of a bill? How does a hen drink?

Wednesday

Talk about *the duck*: How does a duck differ in appearance from a hen? What are young ducks called? How does a duck's bill differ from a hen's bill? How do the feet differ? What can a duck do, that a hen cannot?

Thursday

The turkey: Why is this the favorite bird for the Thanksgiving table? How does the turkey differ in appearance, from the hen? From the duck? What is the male turkey called? Why? Which do you like best to eat—chicken, duck, goose, or turkey?

Friday

Dramatize and play, the story of Chicken Little.

THIRD YEAR

FIRST WEEK

Monday

Rewrite this story in five sentences.

WHY THE CHIPMUNK HAS BLACK STRIPES

Once upon a time the porcupine was made chief of the animals. He called all the animals together for a great council.

The animals seated themselves around a big fire. The porcupine said, "We have a great question to decide. It is this: 'Shall we have daylight all the time or night all the time?'"

All the animals began to talk at once. Some wanted one thing, some another. The bear wanted it to be dark all the time. In his big, deep voice he said, "Always night! Always night!"

The little chipmunk, in a loud, high voice, said, "Day will come! Day will come!"

The council was held at night. While the animals were talking the sun rose. The bear and the other night animals were angry. The chipmunk saw the light coming, and started to run away. The angry bear ran after him and struck him on the back with his paw.

Since then, the chipmunk has always had black stripes on his back, and daylight always follows night.

—*Selected*

Tuesday

Rewrite these sentences, filling the blank spaces:

The chipmunk —— black stripes.
The porcupine said, "We —— a question to decide."
The chipmunk said, "Day —— come."
The bear —— it to be dark.
The council —— held at night.
The chipmunk —— the light coming, and —— to run away.
The angry bear —— him with his paw.

Wednesday

For dictation:

I go to the library every Saturday.
I find a book that I would like to read.
I hand the book and my card to the librarian.
She puts the date on my card.

Thursday

Write a paragraph about the proper manner of sitting. What is the result, if a person has a habit of sitting badly?

Friday

Answer each of the following questions, as a complete sentence:

How many days has November?
In what month is Thanksgiving Day?
Where do the birds go, before winter comes?
In what month does Christmas come?

SECOND WEEK

Monday

Write the following poem on the blackboard, and make it the topic for an oral lesson, discussing how fruit grows on tree and vine; growth of the plants; the likeness of the plants to us; the ethical lesson.

PLANT SONG

O, where do you come from, berries red,
Nuts, apples, and plums, that hang ripe overhead,
Sweet, juicy grapes, with your rich purple hue,
Saying, "Pick us and eat us; we're growing for you"?

O, where do you come from, bright flowers and fair,
That please with your colors and fragrance so rare,
Growing with sunshine or sparkling with dew?
"We are blooming for dear little flowers like you."

Our roots are our mouths, taking food from the ground,
Our leaves are our lungs, breathing air all around;
Our sap, like your blood, our veins courses through—
Don't you think, little children, we're somewhat like you?

Your hearts are the soil, your thoughts are the seeds;
Your lives may become useful plants or foul weeds;
If you think but good thoughts your lives will be true,
For good men and women were once children like you.

—*Nellie M. Brown*

Tuesday

Write a list of the nouns in the "Plant Song."

Wednesday

For dictation:

"He that is slow to anger is better than the mighty: and he that ruleth his spirit than he that taketh a city."

Thursday

Write the following nursery rhyme in large letters, on oak tag. Cut into separate words, and place the words in envelopes, one set for each pupil. The pupils are to place the words on their desks, so as to form the complete rhyme.

Hey, diddle, diddle, the cat and the fiddle:
The cow jumped over the moon:
The little dog laughed to see such sport,
And the dog ran away with the spoon.

Friday

Copy the following sentences, filling the blank spaces:

This —— November.
The birds are —— to the south.
The leaves are —— from the trees.
Thanksgiving —— this month.
Winter —— soon be ——.

THIRD WEEK

Monday

Have the children copy half of the following poem in their composition books:

WHAT THE SNOWBIRDS SAID

"Cheep, cheep," said some little snow-birds,
As the snow came whirling down;
"We haven't a nest,
Or a place to rest,
Save this oak-tree bending down."

"Cheep, cheep," said the little Wee-Wing,

"Cheep, cheep," said the little Wee-Wing,
The smallest bird of all;
"I have never a care,
In the winter air—
God cares for great and small."

"Peep, peep," said her father, Gray-Breast,
"You're a thoughtless bird, my dear,
We all must eat,
And warm our feet,
When snow and ice are here."

"Cheep, cheep," said the little Wee-Wing,
"You are wise and good, I know;
But think of the fun
For each little one,
When we have ice and snow.

"Now I can see, from my perch on the tree,
The merriest, merriest sight—
Boys skating along
On the ice so strong—
Cheep, cheep, how merry and bright!"

"And I see," said the Brownie Snow-bird,
A sight that is prettier far—
Five dear little girls,
With clustering curls,
And eyes as bright as a star."

"And I," said his brother, Bright-Eyes,
"See a man of ice and snow;
He wears a queer hat,
His large nose is flat—
The little boys made him, I know."

"I see some sleds," said Mother Brown,
"All filled with girls and boys;
They laugh and sing,

Their voices ring,
And I like the cheerful noise."

Then the snow-birds all said, "Cheep and chee,
Hurrah for ice and snow;
For the girls and boys,
Who drop us crumbs,
As away to their sport they go!

"Hurrah for the winter, clear and cold,
When the dainty snowflakes fall!
We will sit and sing,
On our oaken swing,
For God takes care of us all!"—*Selected*

Tuesday

Have the children copy the rest of the poem, "What the Snowbirds Said."

Wednesday

Write a list of the nouns in the poem.

Thursday

Write a list of the verbs in the poem.

Friday

Write five sentences, telling what the birds said.

FOURTH WEEK

Monday

Have the pupils tell you the story of Thanksgiving.

Tuesday

Have each child write about something that will be found on the Thanksgiving table, and have the others guess what is described: as pepper, salt, vinegar, bread, sugar, apples, etc.

Wednesday

Story for reproduction:

THE GRUMBLING SNOWFLAKE

The snowflakes were told to go down to the earth to keep it warm. All were glad to go except one. This little snowflake grumbled while the others were getting ready.

"What is the use of going down to that great place?" he said. "I should be glad to keep the plants from freezing, but I never can. I am too small. I could not even cover one speck of that great earth. However, if all the rest of the snowflakes are going, I suppose I shall have to go, too."

The snowflakes had great fun as they fell. They danced and played, and they laughed when they thought they were going to be useful in the great world.

But the grumbling snowflake said, "If I were bigger, I might be of some use!"

One little snowflake reached the earth, and then another. Last of all, the grumbling snowflake came down, too, but he did not see the brown earth. It was all covered with a white snow-blanket.

Every little flake had covered a tiny bit of the brown earth, until the ground was all covered up for the winter.

"I was wrong," said the grumbling snowflake. "I will not grumble again."—*Adapted*

Have the pupils reproduce the story orally.

Thursday

Have the pupils rewrite the story of the grumbling snowflake, in their own words.

Friday

Write a letter to a cousin, telling why you like November.

FOURTH YEAR

FIRST WEEK

Monday

Pass around well-known pictures, if possible, have as many different pictures as there are children. Have each pupil describe his picture.

Tuesday

For dictation:

EVENING HYMN

Now the day is over,
Night is drawing nigh,
Shadows of the evening
Steal across the sky.

Now the darkness gathers,
Stars begin to peep,
Birds and beasts and flowers
Soon will be asleep.
—*S. Baring-Gould*

Wednesday

Original composition, on the signs of coming winter. What signs can be seen in the fields? What about the grass? The leaves? The sky? The birds? The cold?

Thursday

To be read, for written reproduction:

THE WONDERFUL TRAVELING CLOAK

One day a little old woman in gray visited Prince Dolor. She gave him a present.

"What is this?" he asked, as he untied the many knots.

"It is a traveling cloak," she answered.

"Oh," said the little prince, "I never go traveling. Sometimes nurse hoists me on a parapet, but I never go farther than that."

"But this is not an ordinary cloak," said his godmother. "It is a wonderful cloak. It will take you anywhere you wish to go. From it you may see anything you wish to see."

"But how can I get out of the tower?" he asked.

"Open the skylights," she said, "then sit in the middle of the cloak. Say your charm and out you will float through the blue sky on your wonderful cloak."—*From "The Little Lame Prince."*

Friday

Letters of introduction may be sent by mail, or be presented by the person introduced. In the latter case, the letter is never sealed. The envelope is addressed in the usual way, but in the lower left-hand corner is written, "Introducing Mr. Smith, or Miss Smith," as the case may be.

Write the above on the blackboard. Have the pupils look up in the dictionary, and write out definitions of the following words: Introduction, presented, person, latter, addressed, usual, way.

SECOND WEEK

Monday

Write sentences containing the irregular verbs *go, went, gone, see, saw, seen, am, was, been.*

Tuesday

For dictation:

Hail to the merry harvest time,
The gayest of the year:
The time of rich and bounteous crops,
Rejoicing and good cheer.
—*Charles Dickens*

Wednesday

Exercise for clearness of enunciation. Have the following read aloud by every child in turn, each word and syllable to be enunciated clearly.

THE OWL

In the hollow tree, in the old gray tower,
The spectral owl doth dwell;
Dull, hated, despised, in the sunshine hour,
But at dusk he's abroad and well:
Not a bird of the forest e'er mates with him;
All mock him outright by day;
But at night, when the woods grow still and dim,
The boldest will shrink away.
O, when the night falls, and roosts the fowl,
Then, then is the reign of the horned owl!
—*Barry Cornwall*

Thursday

Selection to be memorized:

He prayeth best, who loveth best
  All things both great and small,
For the dear Lord who loveth us,
  He made and loveth all.—*Coleridge*

Friday

Write a letter of introduction for one of your classmates, to be addressed to the principal of the school, or the chairman of the committee of the school district.

THIRD WEEK

Monday

Story for written reproduction:

THE INDIAN CHILDREN

Bright Eyes and Fawn Foot were two little Indian children. They lived in an Indian village near a swift river.

All the people of this village belonged to one family or tribe. The bravest man was the chief. He had the finest wigwam.

One day the Indians moved from the village to a place in the woods. Here they hoped to find game to live on through the winter.

Little Fawn Foot helped her mother when they moved. Bright Eyes was carried on his mother's back. He was too small to help.

When warm weather came they all moved back to the village.

Outline: The Indian children and their home. The tribe. The removal. Fawn Foot and Bright Eyes at the moving. The return.—*Selected*

Tuesday

Write a list of the adjectives in the story, "The Indian children"; a list of the nouns; a list of the verbs.

Wednesday

Write what you see in Boughton's picture, "The Return of the Mayflower."

Thursday

Write about an imaginary journey from London, England, to Boston. How long does it take to cross the ocean? What is the deck of a steamship? What is a stateroom like?

Friday

Write an advertisement asking for a position for yourself.

FOURTH WEEK

Monday

For dictation:

THE GRAINS OF WHEAT

Some grains of wheat lived in a sack. It was so dark that they all went to sleep.

At last the sack was moved. The grains of wheat awoke. They heard some one say, "Take this sack to the mill."

The grains of wheat had a long ride. When they reached the mill a man put them into a hopper. The grains of wheat were crushed between two stones.

—*Selected*

Tuesday

Rewrite in your own words, the story of "The Grains of Wheat."

Wednesday

Write a letter to a friend, telling where wheat grows, how it grows, how flour is made, and how the flour is used.

Thursday

Describe how fire-drills are conducted in your school.

Friday

Talk about the coming of winter, and the indications that are apparent at this time.

DECEMBER

FIRST YEAR

FIRST WEEK

Monday

Story, to be told to the children, and retold by them:

THE WOODPECKER

An old lady lived on a hill.

She was very small, and she always wore a black dress and a large white apron with big bows behind.

On her head she wore the queerest little red bonnet that you ever saw.

The little old lady grew very selfish as the years went by. People said this was because she thought of no one but herself.

One morning as she was baking cakes, a tired, hungry old man came up to her door.

"My good woman," said he, "will you give me one of your cakes? I am very hungry. I have no money, but whatever you first wish for you shall have."

The old lady looked at her cakes and thought that they were too large to give away. So she broke off a small bit of dough and put it into the oven to bake.

When it was done she thought that this one was too nice and brown for a beggar. So she baked a smaller cake, and then a still smaller one, but each came out of the oven as nice and as brown as the first.

At last she took a piece of dough as small as the head of a pin. Even this, when it was baked, was as large and as fine as the others. So the old lady put all the cakes on the shelf and offered the old man a crust of dry bread.

The old man only looked at her, and before the old lady could wink, he was gone.

The old lady thought a great deal about what she had done. She knew it was very wrong.

"I wish I were a bird," she said; "I would fly to him with the largest cake I have."

As she spoke, she felt herself growing smaller and smaller. Suddenly the wind picked her up and carried her up the chimney.

When she came out she still had on her red bonnet and black dress. You could see her white apron with the big bows. But she was a bird, just as she had wished to be.

She was a wise bird, and at once she began to pick her food out of the hard wood of a tree. As people saw her at work, they called her the red-headed woodpecker.

Tuesday

Have the children tell the story of the red-headed woodpecker.

Wednesday

Have the children play the story of the woodpecker as a game.

Thursday

Write the word *woodpecker*.

Friday

Write: *The Woodpecker has a red head.*

SECOND WEEK

Monday

Have the children write the words omitted:

Old —— Hubbard
Went to the —— board
To get her poor —— a bone.
But when she got ——,
The —— board was bare,
And so the poor —— had none.

Tuesday

Have the children give orally all the words they can think of that rhyme with *dog*. Write these in a list on the blackboard, and use them for drills in phonics.

Wednesday

Have the date and the word *December* written by the children.

Thursday

To be committed to memory:

WHAT MAKES CHRISTMAS

Little wishes on white wings,
Little gifts—such tiny things—
Just one little heart that sings,
Make a Merry Christmas.
—*Dorothy Howe*

Friday

Have the children write: *Merry Christmas.*

THIRD WEEK

Monday

To be recited by the teacher and acted out by the children, as a game:

WHEN SANTA CLAUS COMES

Merrily, merrily, merrily, O,
The reindeer prances across the snow;
We hear their tinkling silver bells,
Whose merry music softly tells
Old Santa Claus is coming.

Merrily, merrily, merrily, O,
The evergreens in the woodland grow;
They rustle gently in the breeze;
O, don't you think the Christmas trees
Know Santa Claus is coming?

Merrily, merrily, merrily, O,
We've hung our stockings in a row;
Into our beds we softly creep,
Just shut our eyes and go to sleep—
And wait—for Santa Claus is coming.

—*Selected*

Tuesday

Story for oral reproduction:

BABY BUNTING'S FIRST CHRISTMAS

Baby Bunting was ten months old before she had a Christmas. When the first Christmas came, she didn't know what it meant. When she saw the tree all covered with candles and apples and little baskets of candy, she smiled, and then laughed, and then crowed out loud. She shook her fat hands at the pretty sight, while Father and Mother and Sister Nora danced around her baby carriage.

Then they began to take the presents off the tree. There was a fine clock for Mother and a pair of slippers for Father. Sister Nora had a beautiful doll.

Baby Bunting herself had a warm little muff, some dainty socks, a pair of baby shoes, some picture books, and so many presents besides that it would take too long to tell about them all.

Sister Nora was happy with her big wax doll. She named her Sally Bunting, and brought her to the carriage to make a call on her sister Baby Bunting.

Baby was so pleased at this, that she almost talked. It seemed to Nora as if she really did talk to Sally. Perhaps Sally, the baby doll, could hear this talk better than anyone else.

I am sure Baby Bunting was saying that this was the best Christmas she had seen in ten months.

—Adapted

Wednesday

Have the children tell the story of "Baby Bunting's First Christmas."

Thursday

To be committed to memory:

CHRISTMAS SECRETS

Secrets big and secrets small,
On the eve of Christmas.
Such keen ears has every wall,
That we whisper, one and all,
On the eve of Christmas.

Secrets upstairs, secrets down,
On the eve of Christmas.
Papa brings them from the town,
Wrapped in papers, stiff and brown,
On the eve of Christmas.

But the secret best of all,
On the eve of Christmas,
Steals right down the chimney tall,
Fills our stockings one and all,
On the eve of Christmas.

—Alice E. Allen

Friday

Help the children to learn "Christmas Secrets."

FOURTH WEEK

Monday

Let the children play, as a game, "Christmas Secrets."

Tuesday

Continue learning the poem. Have the children write: *Secrets big and secrets small.*

Wednesday

Have each child name something that he would like or that he had for Christmas. Write these in a list on the blackboard, the simplest of them to be read afterwards by the little folks.

Thursday

Talk about what the children did on Christmas Day.

Friday

Talk with the children about winter; the close of the old year, and the coming of the new year.

SECOND YEAR

FIRST WEEK

Monday

For dictation:

Sing soft! sing low!
The time of the snow
Is December.

Tuesday

Talk about the beginning of winter. What is the first month of winter? What are the three winter months? What was the month before December? What are the three autumn months? What season follows winter? What are the three spring months? What season follows spring? What are the three summer months? How many days are there in December?

Wednesday

For drill in phonics, or for clear enunciation:

There was a man and his name was Pat,
He had a wife and her name was Mat;
He had a rat and she had a cat;
The cat was Mat's and the rat was Pat's.
They all lived together,
In all kinds of weather,
Pat's rat and Mat's cat,
Cat, rat, Mat and Pat.

Thursday

To be committed to memory:

A CHRISTMAS VISIT

When the children sound are sleeping,
And the night is cold and clear;
When the frost-elves watch are keeping,

Some one comes our hearts to cheer.
Fast he drives his reindeer prancing;
No one hears his sleigh-bells ring,
No one sees him soft advancing,
No one knows what he will bring.

He's a jolly soul, and merry,
With his cheeks an autumn hue,
And his nose is like a cherry
While he's looking round for you.
If he hears a child awaking,
Quickly then he slips from sight,
But if all a nap are taking
Then he works away till light.

Once a boy who was not sleeping,
On Christmas morn stole through the hall;
Slow and silent he went creeping,
But no stocking found at all.
And a girl who tiptoed, peeping
Into rooms, and up the stair,
In the morning they found weeping,
For no Santa had been there.

So, when merry folk you're greeting,
And you long to strip your tree,
When old Santa you'd be meeting,
Wait, nor hurry down to see;
For if you should hunt him early,
Maybe he'd not come next year;
He would be so cross and surly
That he'd pass your house, I fear.

—*Mabel L. Gray*

Have the first two stanzas copied by the children.

Friday

Have the children copy the second two stanzas of "A Christmas Visit."

SECOND WEEK

Monday

Pupils learn first stanza of "A Christmas Visit."

Tuesday

Pupils learn second stanza of the poem.

Wednesday

Pupils learn third stanza of the poem.

Thursday

Pupils learn fourth stanza of the poem.

Friday

Have the pupils recite the entire poem in concert.

THIRD WEEK

Monday

Pupils write a list of the naming words (nouns) in "A Christmas Visit."

Tuesday

For dictation:

All that's great and good is done done—
Just by trying.

Wednesday

Story for reproduction:

THE SUNBEAMS

The Sun was up.

The sky in the east had told that he was on the way, for it had turned red and gold as he came near. He looked down on the earth, and there was a new day. So he sent out his beams to wake everybody from sleep.

A beam came to the little birds in the trees, and they rose at once. They flew about, singing as loudly as they could.

Then a beam came and waked the rabbit. He gave his eyes a rub and ran out into the green field to eat grass.

Another beam came into the hen-house. The rooster flapped his wings and crowed. The hens flew into the yard to see what they could find to eat.

A beam came to the beehive. A bee came out of the hive. He flew off to the fields to drink honey from the flowers.

The beam that came to Johnny's bed awakened Johnny, but the boy would not get up. He went to sleep once more, though all the animals were up, and hard at work.—*Adapted*

Thursday

Have the children tell, in their own words, the story of "The Sunbeams."

Friday

Children write five sentences, telling what the sunbeams did.

FOURTH WEEK

Monday

Talk with the little folks about Christmas, its meaning, and the beauty of giving.

Tuesday

Have each child write three things he would like for Christmas.

Wednesday

Pupils tell what they did on Christmas Day.

Thursday

Talk about the year's holidays. How many are there? What are they?

Friday

Children write a letter to a cousin, telling what they did on Christmas Day.

THIRD YEAR

FIRST WEEK

Monday

To be committed to memory:

THE WIND AND THE MOON

Said the Wind to the Moon, "I will blow you out.
You stare
In the air
Like a ghost in a chair,
Always looking what I am about;
I hate to be watched; I will blow you out."

The Wind blew hard, and out went the Moon,
So deep,
On a heap
Of clouds, to sleep,
Down lay the Wind, and slumbered soon—
Muttering low, “I’ve done for that Moon.”

He turned in his bed; she was there again!
On high,
In the sky,
With her one ghost eye,
The Moon shone white and alive and plain,
Said the Wind—”I will blow you out again.”

The Wind blew hard, and the Moon grew dim,
With my sledge
And my wedge
I have knocked off her edge!
If only I blow right fierce and grim,
The creature will soon be dimmer than dim.

He blew and blew, and she thinned to a thread,
One puff
More’s enough
To blow her to snuff!
One good puff more where the last was bred,
And glimmer, glimmer, glum will go the thread!

He blew a great blast and the thread was gone;
In the air
Nowhere
Was a moonbeam bare;
Far off and harmless the shy stars shone;
Sure and certain the Moon was gone!

The Wind he took to his revels once more;
On down,
In town,

Like a merry mad clown,
He leaped and hallooed with whistle and war.
What's that? The glimmering thread once more!

But the Moon she knew nothing about the affair,
For, high
In the sky,
With her one white eye,
Motionless, miles above the air,
She had never heard the great Wind blare.
—*George Macdonald*

Have the first half of the poem copied.

Tuesday

Have the rest of the poem copied.

Wednesday

Have the children commit to memory the first two stanzas of the poem.

Thursday

Children commit to memory the second two stanzas of the poem.

Friday

Children learn the fifth and sixth stanzas of the poem.

SECOND WEEK

Monday

Children learn the seventh and eighth stanzas of "The Wind and the Moon."

Tuesday

Children learn the rest of the poem.

Wednesday

Children recite the entire poem.

Thursday

Children recite the poem. Write a list of the nouns in the poem.

Friday

Write a list of the doing words (verbs) in the poem.

THIRD WEEK

Monday

For dictation:

Little fairy snowflakes,
   Dancing in the flue;
Old Mr. Santa Claus,
   What is keeping you?

Tuesday

Write a list of as many words rhyming with *time*, as you can think of.

Wednesday

Conversation about Christmas.

Thursday

Write five sentences about Christmas.

Friday

Children write a list of Christmas presents suitable for a boy, a list of presents suitable for a girl.

FOURTH WEEK

Monday

Story for reproduction:

A CLOUD STORY

A long time ago, there lived a wonderful king. Each day this king came in his golden chariot, bringing light, heat, and happiness to all the people.

Each day he passed from his palace in the east to his throne in the west. He never missed a day, for he wanted to make sure that everyone had a share of his gifts.

For everybody, he had the birds sing and the flowers bloom. For everybody, he showed beautiful pictures, which changed every hour.

The king had many beautiful daughters. They were often called swan maidens, because they rode upon beautiful white swans.

When the swan maidens were with their father they wore soft white or gray dresses.

Sometimes the king saw that the grass was brown, or the buds were not coming out. Then he said, “Swan maidens, who will go and work to-day?”

Almost before he was through speaking, many of them had rushed away. Sometimes more of them came than could work upon the grass and buds.

Then some of them ran off to play. But the best of them went down to feed the roots and the worms. They worked out of sight.

But they always went back to their father, the king.

Now it is very hard work to catch a swan maiden on her way back home.

A boy is sure he saw one of them on a ring in the tea-kettle steam. How many of them get away is a secret.

When the king saw the flowers shiver in the fall, he called the bravest swan maidens to him. He told them that they must go away for a long time.

Then each swan maiden put on a beautiful white dress, and came softly down, down to earth, with a warm blanket.

These blankets they spread over the flowers and seeds. Every little flower went to sleep under the blanket.

At last the king smiled, and their work was done. They slipped away home so softly that nobody missed them, but the boys and girls who loved the snow.

—*Adapted*

Tuesday

Children tell "A Cloud Story" in their own words.

Wednesday

Children write the cloud story.

Thursday

Children write five sentences about snow.

Friday

Children write what they did on Christmas Day.

FOURTH YEAR

FIRST WEEK

Monday

To be committed to memory:

SWEET AND LOW

Sweet and low, sweet and low,
   Wind of the western sea,
Low, low, breathe and blow,
   Wind of the western sea!
Over the rolling waters go;
Come from the dying moon and blow,
   Blow him again to me;
While my little one, while my pretty one, sleeps.

Sleep and rest, sleep and rest,
   Father will come to thee soon.
Rest, rest on mother's breast,
   Father will come to thee soon.
Father will come to his babe in the nest;
Silver sails all out of the west,
   Under the silver moon;
Sleep, my little one, sleep, my pretty one, sleep!

—*Alfred Tennyson*

Have the poem copied.

Tuesday

Pupils learn first stanza of the poem.

Wednesday

Pupils learn the entire poem.

Thursday

Write about the life of Alfred Tennyson.

Friday

Write in complete sentences answers to the following questions:

How is the sea to blow?
Where is the wind to go?
Where is the wind to come from?
What is the blowing of the wind to do?
What is the baby to do?
When will father come?
Where is the baby to rest?
Where will father come?
How will father come?

SECOND WEEK

Monday

Write a letter, addressed to Santa Claus, telling what you would like for Christmas.

Tuesday

Write a telegram of ten words, saying that you will go to some special place for Christmas.

Wednesday

Write the abbreviations for the days of the week and the months of the year.

Thursday

Have the children dramatize, in their own way:

Old King Cole
Was a merry old soul,
And a merry old soul was he.
He called for his pipe,
He called for his bowl,
And he called for his fiddlers three.

Friday

For dictation:

Beautiful hands are those that do
Work that is earnest and brave and true,
Moment by moment, the long day through.

THIRD WEEK

Monday

Talk about the signs of winter.

Tuesday

Pupils write about signs of winter.

Wednesday

Write a rhyme of two lines, containing the word *snow*.

Thursday

Talk about winter sports.

Friday

Write about winter sports.

FOURTH WEEK

Monday

For dictation:

> He prayeth best, who loveth best,
>   All things both great and small;
> For the dear God who loveth us,
>   He made and loveth all.

Tuesday

Every child find a short quotation for some other pupil to read in class.

Wednesday

Write letters, telling why you like Christmas.

Thursday

Write a composition on snow.

Friday

Have a spelling match.

JANUARY

FIRST YEAR

FIRST WEEK

Monday

Talk about the new year. What is this month called? What was last month? What is the name of the new year? What was the name of the last year? How many days has January? What season is this? What are the months of the winter season? What season comes after winter?

Tuesday

Write the word *January*; also the date.

Wednesday

To be taught to the children:

Sixty seconds make a minute,
Something sure you can learn in it;
Sixty minutes make an hour,
Work with all your might and power;
Twenty-four hours make a day,
Time enough for work and play.
Seven days a week will make;
You will learn, if pains you take.—*Selected*

Thursday

Practise learning the rhyme of the day before.

Friday

Write: *Seven days make a week.*

SECOND WEEK

Monday

Write:

On Monday, when the weather is fair,
I always wash the clothes.

Tuesday

Write:

On Tuesday I can iron them,
Even if it rains and snows.

Wednesday

Write:

On Wednesday I do all the mending,
I like the mending too.

Thursday

Write:

On Thursday I receive my friends;
I have nothing else to do.

Friday

Write:

Friday is the time to sweep,
To dust, and set things right.

The teacher may recite the following to the children, then have the entire poem of the week played as a game, with appropriate actions:

On Saturday I always cook,
Then put all work from sight.

And Sunday is the day of rest;
I go to church dressed in my best.
—*Selected*

THIRD WEEK

Monday

Learn the names of the months, by having a procession of children representing the various months, led by the New Year. The little folks will enjoy the game, and will learn the names of the twelve months, in their order, without realizing that they are doing anything but play.

Tuesday

Story poem, to be recited (or read, if needs must) to the children, by the teacher:

A MYSTERY

I put my coat and furs and mittens on, to go
With my cunning Christmas sled, out to see the pretty snow.

I made some little balls, and they looked as white and nice—
I tried how one would taste, but it was just as cold as ice.

I took some to the kitchen then, because I thought, you see,
I'd bake them just like apples—they'd be good with cream and tea.

I didn't say a single word about it to the cook,
When I put them in the oven, but when she gave a look,

She stared, and held her hands up, and said: "For pity's sake!
Who put this water in here, and spoiled my ginger cake?"

I couldn't tell. It wasn't I; but I would like to know,
Where did my pretty apples, that I was baking, go?

—*Selected*

After reciting the poem, ask the children what became of the snow apples.

Wednesday

Talk about snow; snowballs; sliding on the snow; sleighing; a snow man.

Thursday

Write: *I can make a snowball.*

Friday

To be told; for the children to guess:

WHAT AM I?

I live in a hole just above somebody's chin. I have to stay there, for I am fastened in.

It is because of me that boys and girls like good things to eat. To please me, they eat candy and fruit.

It is because of me that boys and girls are often kept after school. They forget, and use me when they ought not to.

I am always wanting to taste, taste, taste. I am always wanting to talk, talk, talk.

Who can guess what I am?

FOURTH WEEK

Monday

Children write the words necessary to complete the following:

Jack and ——
Went up the ——,
To get a —— of water.
—— fell down
And —— his crown,
And —— came tumbling after.

Tuesday

Have the children give all the words they can that rhyme with *hat*. Write the list on the blackboard, and use it for drill in phonics.

Wednesday

To be taught to the children:

If you can't be the big sun, with his cheery smile,
You can be the cheerful sunbeam for a little while.

Thursday

Play "I am thinking of something," using objects in the school-room.

Friday

Have the children mention as many objects as they can think of that are blue; green; yellow; white.

SECOND YEAR

FIRST WEEK

Monday

To be committed to memory:

LADY MOON

Lady Moon, Lady Moon, where are you roving?
"Over the sea."
Lady Moon, Lady Moon, whom are you loving?
"All that love me."

Are you not tired with roving and never
Resting to sleep?
Why look so pale and so sad, as forever
Wishing to weep?

"Ask me not this, little child, if you love me:
You are too bold.
I must obey my dear Father above me,
And do as I'm told."

Lady Moon, Lady Moon, where are you roving?
"Over the sea."
Lady Moon, Lady Moon, whom are you loving?
"All that love me."

—Lord Houghton

Have the first stanza of the poem copied and learned.

Tuesday

Have the second stanza of the poem copied and learned.

Wednesday

Have the third stanza of the poem copied and learned.

Thursday

Have the fourth stanza of the poem copied and learned.

Friday

Have the poem recited, throughout.

SECOND WEEK

Monday

For dictation:

> Be kind in all you say and do,
> That others may be kind to you.

Tuesday

Talk about snowflakes; if possible, showing some of the single flakes. Where do the snowflakes come from? What becomes of them if they are taken into a warm room? What becomes of them when they fall? What becomes of the snow when the weather gets warm? How does the snow help the grass and flowers? (Keeps them warm during the cold winter.) Why is snow sometimes called a blanket?

Wednesday

Story for oral reproduction:

A WISE DOG

One night a farmer was riding home along a lane which had walls on both sides. Suddenly he heard his dog barking on the farther side of the wall.

The man stopped his horse and started to see what was the matter.

The night was very cold. Snow lay on the ground. Sitting on a large stone was the farmer's little daughter.

The child had left the house and had wandered out into the meadow.

The dog had followed her, keeping close at her heels. Now he was barking for some one to come and take the little girl home. She had lost her way, and was crying.

The father looked at the footprints in the snow. He saw that his little daughter had walked close beside a deep hole.

She had walked all the way round the hole. But the wise dog had gone, all the time, between the little girl and the great hole.

Was he not a wise dog?—*Adapted*

Thursday

Children tell the story of the lost child and the dog.

Friday

Write three sentences about the little girl and the dog.

THIRD WEEK

Monday

Supply words to fill the following blanks:

My dog Spot is ——.
He eats ——.
Spot can ——.
When I run, Spot —— too.

Tuesday

To be committed to memory:

Hearts, like doors, will ope with ease,
To very, very little keys;
And don't forget that two of these
Are, "Thank you, sir," and "If you please."
—*Selected*

Wednesday

Write a list of ten objects to be seen in the school-room.

Thursday

Talk about bread. Who makes the bread we eat? What is it made of? Where does the flour come from? Where does wheat grow? How does wheat grow? How is the wheat made into flour? How is the flour made into bread?

Friday

Write three sentences about bread.

FOURTH WEEK

Monday

Children write their fathers' and mothers' names.

Tuesday

For dictation:

> When the cold wind blows,
> Look out for your nose.

Wednesday

Talk about how we are protected from cold, by clothing and by artificial heat. How is the school-room warmed? How are the children's homes warmed? Why is it unnecessary for stables to be heated?

Thursday

A riddle for the children to guess:

> I am as black, as black can be,
>   But yet I shine.
> My home was deep within the earth,
>   In a dark mine.
> Years ago I was buried there,
>   And yet I hold
> The sunshine and the heat, which warmed
>   That world of old.
> Though black and cold I seem to be,
>   Yet I can glow.
> Just put me on a blazing fire—
>   Then you will know.—*Selected*

Friday

Write three sentences about coal.

THIRD YEAR

FIRST WEEK

Monday

To be committed to memory:

CHILD'S EVENING PRAYER

Now the day is over,
  Night is drawing nigh;
Shadows of the evening
  Steal across the sky.

Low the darkness gathers,
  Stars begin to peep;
Birds and beasts and flowers
  Soon will be asleep.

Through the long night-watches,
  May Thine angels spread
Their white wings above me,
  Watching round my bed.

When the morn awakens,
  Then may I arise,
Pure and fresh and sinless,
  In Thy holy eyes.—*S. Baring-Gould*

Have the poem copied.

Tuesday

Learn the first verse of the poem.

Wednesday

Learn the rest of the poem.

Thursday

Recite the entire poem.

Friday

Write a list of the naming words (nouns) in the "Child's Evening Prayer."

SECOND WEEK

Monday

Write a list of the doing words (verbs), in the "Child's Evening Prayer."

Tuesday

Write a letter to a playmate, telling what you did on a recent Saturday.

Wednesday

For dictation:

> Boats sail on the rivers,
>   And ships sail on the seas,
> But clouds that sail across the sky
>   Are prettier far than these.—*Selected*

Thursday

Write five sentences about clouds.

Friday

Write a list of ten objects that are blue.

THIRD WEEK

Monday

Each child write eight sentences, describing some other child in the room, telling: Color of hair, color of eyes, kind of complexion, height (guessed at), age, costume worn, size of shoes (guessed at), and size of gloves.

Tuesday

Write a rhyme of four lines about a dog.

Wednesday

Write a list of the objects to be seen in the school-room. Who can write the longest list?

Thursday

Have the following poem copied:

WINTER EVENING

What way does the wind come? Which way does he go?
He rides over the water, and over the snow,
Through wood, and through vale; and o'er rocky height,
Which the great cannot climb, takes his sounding flight;

He tosses about in every bare tree,
As, if you look up, you may plainly see;
But how he will come, and whither he goes,
There's never a scholar anywhere knows.

He will suddenly stop in a cunning nook,
And ring a sharp 'larum; but, if you should look,
There's nothing to see but a cushion of snow,
Round as a pillow, and whiter than milk,
And softer than if it were covered with silk.

Sometimes he'll hide in the cave of the rock,
Then whistle as shrill as a cuckoo clock.
Yet seek him—and what shall you find in his place?
Nothing but silence and empty space;
Save, in a corner, a heap of dry leaves,
That he's left, for a bed, to beggars or thieves!

—*Dorothy Wordsworth*

Friday

Pupils write a list of the nouns in the poem, "Winter Evening."

FOURTH WEEK

Monday

Pupils write a list of the verbs in the poem, "Winter Evening."

Tuesday

Write five sentences telling what the wind does.

Wednesday

Children find answers to the following questions, in any way they can:

What little children wear wooden shoes?
What little children wear moccasins?
What little children wear shoes of fur?
What children wear shoes of silk or satin?
What children wear shoes of leather?

Thursday

Write five sentences about the different kinds of shoes children wear.

Friday

Write five sentences about the shoes you have on.

FOURTH YEAR

FIRST WEEK

Monday

To be committed to memory:

SONG OF THE BROOK

I come from haunts of coot and hern,
 I make a sudden sally,
And sparkle out among the fern
 To bicker down a valley.

By thirty hills I hurry down,
   Or slip between the ridges,
By twenty thorps, a little town
   And half a hundred bridges.

Till last by Philip's farm I flow,
   To join the brimming river,
For men may come and men may go,
   But I go on forever.

I chatter over stony ways,
   In little sharps and trebles,
I bubble into eddying bays,
   I babble on the pebbles.

With many a curve my banks I fret
   By many a field and fallow,
And many a fairy foreland set
   With willow weed and mallow.

I chatter, chatter, as I flow
   To join the brimming river;
For men may come and men may go,
   But I go on forever.

I wind about, and in and out,
   With here a blossom sailing,
And here and there a lusty trout,
   And here and there a grayling.

And here and there a foamy flake
   Upon me, as I travel,
With many a silvery water-break,
   Above the golden gravel.

And draw them all along, and flow
   To join the brimming river,
For men may come and men may go,
   But I go on forever.

I steal by lawns and grassy plots,
  I slide by hazel covers;
I move the sweet forget-me-nots
  That grow for happy lovers.

I slip, I slide, I gloom, I glance
  Among my skimming swallows;
I make the melted sunbeams glance
  Against my sandy shallows.

I murmur under moon and stars
  In brambly wildernesses;
I linger by my shingly bars—
  I loiter round my cresses.

And out again I curve and flow
  To join the brimming river,
For men may come and men may go,
  But I go on forever.—*Alfred Tennyson*

Have the first six stanzas of the poem copied.

Tuesday

Have the rest of the poem copied.

Wednesday

Pupils commit to memory the first three stanzas of the poem.

Thursday

Commit to memory the second three stanzas of the poem.

Friday

Commit to memory the third three stanzas of the poem.

SECOND WEEK

Monday

Commit to memory the rest of the poem.

Tuesday

Recite the entire poem.

Wednesday

Study up the life of Alfred Tennyson.

Thursday

Answer the following questions:

Where does the brook come from?
What is a "coot"? (See dictionary.)
What is a "hern"? (See dictionary.)
What does the brook do among the ferns?
What is meant by the brook's "bickering"?
How does the brook come down by thirty hills?
What is meant by the brook's "slipping" between the ridges?
What is a "thorp"?

Friday

Answer the following questions:

What is meant by a "brimming river"?
How does the brook join the river?
How does the brook go on forever?

How does the brook get the water to keep on flowing forever?
What is meant by the brook's "chattering"?
What causes the noises of the brook?
What are "sharps and trebles"?
What is an "eddying bay"? What is an eddy?

THIRD WEEK

Monday

Answer the following questions:

What is the meaning of "fret"?
How does the brook fret the banks with its curves?
What is a "foreland"?
What is "willow-weed"?
What is "mallow"?
What makes the brook wind about?
How do blossoms happen to be sailing on the water?
Whereabouts in the brook do the trout stay?
What is a "grayling"?

Tuesday

Answer the following questions:

What is a "water-break"?
What is "gravel"?
Why is the gravel called golden?
What are some of the things that the brook carries along to the river?
What is meant by "hazel covers"?
Why are the forget-me-nots said to "grow for happy lovers"?

Wednesday

Answer the following questions:

How does the brook go?
What is meant by “skimming” swallows?
What makes the sunbeam in the woods “netted”?
What is a “shallow”?
How does the brook murmur?
What is a “bramble”?
What are “cresses”? Where do they grow?

Thursday

Write in a list all the verbs in the poem.

Friday

Write a list of all the adjectives in the poem.

FOURTH WEEK

Monday

Write a composition on brooks.

Tuesday

Talk about brooks, rivers, and the ocean.

Wednesday

Write a rhyme of four lines about a river.

Thursday

Each pupil find and repeat in class a quotation about a brook, a river, or the ocean.

Friday

Play, “My ship came from China, and it brought to me.”

FEBRUARY

FIRST YEAR

FIRST WEEK

Monday

Talk about the new month. What is this month? What was last month? What month follows February? What season is this? What are the three months of the winter season? What season follows winter? What are the three months of the spring season? What season follows spring? What season follows summer?

Tuesday

To be taught to the children:

Red, white, and blue is our country's flag,
  Flag of the brave and free;
Red, white and blue, where'er you go,
  Is the flag for you and me.—*Selected*

Wednesday

Talk about the flag. How many colors has our flag? What are they? How many red stripes are there? How many white stripes? Where is the blue of the flag? What is there on the blue? Count the stars. How many stars are there?

Thursday

Tell the story of Betsy Ross, and the making of the first United States flag.

Friday

Have the children repeat to you the story of Betsy Ross and the flag. Have the flag salute given. In case the children are not familiar with it, here is the salute usually given:

> "We give our heads, our hearts, and our hands to our country.
> One country, one language, one flag."

During the salute, the flag should be held, unfurled, by some one facing the class. The children point with the right hands to their heads and their hearts. At the words, "our hands," both hands should be extended. At the words "one flag," the right hand only is extended.

SECOND WEEK

Monday

Tell stories of the boyhood of Abraham Lincoln.

Tuesday

Talk about Lincoln's boyhood, allowing the children to tell you the stories which they heard the day before.

Wednesday

Talk about St. Valentine's Day. What do we give on that day? To whom do we give valentines? (To those we love.)

Thursday

Tell the story of good St. Valentine.

Friday

Have the children repeat to you the story of St. Valentine.

THIRD WEEK

Monday

Tell the story of Washington and the hatchet. Remember that, old and stale as the story may be to you, it is new once to every child.

Tuesday

Play, as a game, Washington and his hatchet.

Wednesday

Tell the story of Washington as a general; how he led the armies that fought to make our country free. Tell about his birthday, February 22, and how we celebrate it, in memory of what he did for us.

Thursday

Write: *George Washington, the father of his country.*

Friday

Write: *We live in the United States.*

FOURTH WEEK

Monday

To be taught to the children:

Rainy days and sunny days,
  What difference makes the weather,
When little hearts are full of love,
  And all are glad together.—*Selected*

Tuesday

Tell the children the story of “The Three Bears.”

Wednesday

Have the children tell you the story of “The Three Bears.”

Thursday and Friday

Play the story of “The Three Bears,” as a game.

SECOND YEAR

FIRST WEEK

Monday

To be committed to memory:

THE SHORTEST MONTH

Will the winter never be over,
  Will the dark days never go?
Must the buttercup and the clover
  Be always under the snow?

Ah, lend me your little ear, love,
  Hark! 'tis a beautiful thing;
The dreariest month of the year, love,
  Is shortest and nearest to spring.
—A. D. T. Whitney

Have the poem copied.

Tuesday

Teach the poem to the children.

Wednesday

Supply words to fill the blank spaces in the following:

The Queen of ——,
She made some ——.
All on a summer's ——.
The —— of hearts,
He stole those ——,
And quickly —— away.

Thursday

Story for reproduction:

LINCOLN'S FIRST DOLLAR

When Abraham Lincoln was a boy he went down the river in a boat to carry a load of truck to market. He stood by the river bank, after he had sold his bacon and vegetables. A steamboat was coming down the river.

Two men who wished to go on board the steamer asked Abraham to row them out. He did so, and as they climbed on board they left in his hand two half dollars.

It was the first money he had ever earned, and Abraham was a very proud, happy boy.

Friday

Children tell the story of Abraham Lincoln's first money.

SECOND WEEK

Monday

Teach the following poem to the children:

NED'S CHOICE

She has not rosy cheeks,
Nor eyes that brightly shine,
Nor golden curls, nor teeth like pearls,
This Valentine of thine;
But, oh! she's just the dearest,
The truest and the best,
And one more kind you will not find
In many a long day's quest.

Her cheeks are faded now,
Her dear old eyes are dim;
Her hair's like snow, her steps are slow,
Her figure isn't trim;
But, oh! and, oh! I love her,
This grandmamma of mine;
I wish that she for years may be
My own dear Valentine.—*Selected*

Tuesday

Write three sentences about your grandmother if you have one; if not, about your mother.

Wednesday

Valentine verses, for the children to copy:

I wish I were the tiny cup,
  From which you take your tea;
For every time you took a sip,
  You'd give a kiss to me.

If you love me as I love you,
No knife can cut our love in two.

The rose is red,
  The violet's blue;
Pinks are pretty,
  And so are you.

Wednesday

Write a letter, that might be sent to your mother as a valentine.

Thursday

For dictation:

'Twas a tortoise,
  All yellow and black;
He walked away,
  And never came back.—*Selected*

Friday

Play "The Queen of Hearts" as a game.

THIRD WEEK

Monday

Write a list of words that rhyme with *queen*.

Tuesday

Tell the children the story of Washington and his colt.

Wednesday

Write five sentences about Washington.

Thursday

Tell the story of Washington crossing the Delaware.

Friday

Play, as a game, Washington and his colt, and also Washington crossing the Delaware.

FOURTH WEEK

Monday

Write five sentences about playing in the snow.

Tuesday

Talk about what we eat. Who likes sweet things? Who likes pickles? Who likes meat? Who likes potatoes? Tell the children about foods that they need to eat to be well.

Wednesday

Write a list of things that we eat.

Thursday

Talk about clothing. Why we wear woolen clothing in cold weather; where the wool comes from; talk about sheep.

Friday

Write five sentences about clothing, and where the wool comes from.

THIRD YEAR

FIRST WEEK

Monday

To be committed to memory:

OUR FLAG

There are many flags in many lands,
There are flags of every hue,
But there is no flag in any land,
Like our own Red, White, and Blue.

I know where the prettiest colors are,
I'm sure if I only knew
How to get them here, I could make a flag,
Of glorious Red, White, and Blue.

I could cut a piece from the evening sky,
Where the stars were shining through,
And use it just as it was on high,
For my Stars and field of Blue.

Then I'd want a piece of fleecy cloud,
And some from a rainbow bright,
And I'd put them together, side by side,
For my Stripes of Red and White.

Then "Hurrah for the Flag!" our country's flag,
Its stripes, and white stars, too;
There is no flag in any land,
Like our own Red, White and Blue.—*Selected*

Have the poem copied.

Tuesday

Learn the first two stanzas of the poem.

Wednesday

Learn the rest of the poem.

Thursday

Recite the entire poem.

Friday

Write a list of the nouns, and another of the verbs, in the poem.

SECOND WEEK

Monday

Write a four-line verse suitable for a valentine.

Tuesday

Write the story of St. Valentine.

Wednesday

Talk about Lincoln.

Thursday

Write what you know about Lincoln.

Friday

For dictation:

Twilight and firelight,
  Shadows come and go;
Merry chimes of sleighbells
  Tinkling through the snow;
Mother knitting stockings
  (Pussy's got the ball)—
Don't you think that winter's
  Pleasanter than all?—*Selected*

THIRD WEEK

Monday

Write the story of Washington and the hatchet.

Tuesday

Write three sentences, telling why we should admire Washington.

Wednesday

Tell the story of Lafayette's part in aiding our fight for freedom.

Thursday

Write what you know of Lafayette.

For dictation:

God make my life a little song,
That comforteth the sad;
That helpeth others to be strong,
And makes the singer glad.
—*Selected*

FOURTH WEEK

Monday

Story for reproduction:

THE ROBIN'S RED BREAST

Long ago, in the far north, where it is very cold, there was only one fire.

An old man and his little son took care of this fire and kept it burning day and night.

They knew that if the fire went out all the people would freeze and that the white bear would have the northland all to himself.

But one day the old man became very sick so that his son had everything to do.

For many days and nights he bravely took care of his father and kept the fire burning.

But at last he got so tired and sleepy that he could no longer work.

Now the white bear was always watching the fire.

He longed for the time when he would have the northland all to himself.

And when he saw how tired and sleepy the little boy was, he stayed close to the fire and laughed to himself.

One night the poor little boy could endure no longer and fell fast asleep.

Then the white bear ran as fast as he could and jumped upon the fire with his wet feet and rolled upon it.

At last he thought it was all out and went happily away to his cave.

But a gray robin was flying near and saw what the white bear was doing.

She waited until the bear went away.

Then she flew down and searched with her sharp little eyes until she found a tiny live spark.

This she fanned patiently for a long time with her wings.

Her little breast was scorched red, but she did not give up.

After awhile a fine red blaze sprang up again.

Then she flew away to every hut in the northland.

And everywhere that she touched the ground a fire began to burn.

So that soon instead of one little fire the whole northland was lighted up.

And now all that the white bear could do was to go farther back into his cave and growl.

For now, indeed, he knew that the northland was not all for him.

And this is the reason why the people in the north country love the robin. And they are never tired of telling their children how it got its red breast.

Tuesday

Write the story of the Robin's Red Breast.

Wednesday

Play, as a game, the story of Robin.

Thursday

Write five sentences about birds.

Friday

For dictation:

Two hands and only one mouth have you,
And it is worth while repeating,
That two are for the work you will have to do;
The one is enough for eating.—*Selected*

FOURTH YEAR

FIRST WEEK

Monday

To be committed to memory:

"The Wreck of the Hesperus," by Henry W. Longfellow.

Copy eleven stanzas of the poem.

Tuesday

Copy the rest of the poem.

Wednesday

Learn the first four stanzas of the poem.

Thursday

Learn the second four stanzas of the poem.

Friday

Learn the third four stanzas of the poem.

SECOND WEEK

Monday

Learn the fourth four stanzas of the poem.

Tuesday

Learn the fifth four stanzas of the poem.

Wednesday

Finish learning the poem, and recite it throughout.

Thursday

Recite the poem, and answer the following:

What is a "schooner"? (See dictionary.)

How does the sea in winter differ from a summer sea?

Who was the "skipper"?

Write a description of the captain's daughter.

What is a "helm"?

What is meant by the "veering flaw?"

What did the changing positions of the wind indicate with regard to the weather?

Friday

Where was the "Spanish Main"?

What is a "port"?

What is a "hurricane"?

What does a golden ring around the moon indicate?

Did you ever see one?

What is a "whiff"?

What is a "gale"?

What is meant by the "brine"?

What is meant by "smote amain"?

How could a boat leap?

THIRD WEEK

Monday

What is a "blast"? How could it sting?

What is a "spar"?

What is a "mast"?

What is a "fog-bell"?

What is meant by a “rock-bound coast”?
What guns could be heard?
Why was the sea “angry”?
Where is Norman’s Woe? Why is it so called?

Tuesday

What is a “gust”?
Why was the surf called “trampling”?
What is the bow of a boat?
What is a “wreck”?
Why were the frozen seamen like icicles?

Wednesday

Why did the waves look “fleecy”?
What is “carded wool”?
Why were the rocks called “cruel”?
What is a “shroud”?
What is meant by “went by the board”?
What became of the ship?
What is a “reef”?

Thursday

Look up the life of the poet Longfellow and talk about him.

Friday

Write the story of Longfellow’s life.

FOURTH WEEK

Monday

Write the story of St. Valentine.

Tuesday

Write the story of Lincoln’s boyhood.

Wednesday

Write about what Washington did for our country.

Thursday

Talk about patriotism; what it means, and how we can best show our patriotism.

Friday

Write the story of the making of the first American flag.

MARCH

FIRST YEAR

FIRST WEEK

Monday

Talk about the new month. What month is this? What was last month? What month follows March? What season is this? What are the three months of the spring season? What season follows spring? What season is just past? How many days has March? What is March sometimes called? (The windy month.)

Tuesday

Write the date. Write the word *March*.

Wednesday

Talk about the wind. Can we see the wind? How do we know when the wind is blowing? What does the wind do to the trees? What does it do to the clothes hanging on the line? What does it do to our faces? (Makes our cheeks rosy.)

Thursday

To be taught to the children:

WHO HAS SEEN THE WIND?

Who has seen the wind?
Neither I nor you;
But when the leaves hang trembling
The wind is passing through.

Who has seen the wind?
Neither you nor I,
But when the trees bow down their heads
The wind is passing by.
—Christina Rossetti

Friday

Teach the children the poem given above.

SECOND WEEK

Monday

Talk about wind-mills: How they are used; how they turn; Holland and the wind-mills of that country.

Tuesday

Write:

Who has seen the wind?
Neither you nor I.

Wednesday

Story to be told to the children:

THE WINDS

This is one of the stories that the fathers and mothers in Greece used to tell their children.

Æolus was the father of all the winds, great and small. He had six sons and six daughters.

When the children were old enough, they went out into the world to work. Often they were gone all day long.

They had to sweep and dust the whole world. They carried water from the sea to wash and scrub the earth.

They helped to move the great ships across the ocean. They scattered the seeds, and watered the flowers, and did many other helpful things.

And these things are what the winds do for us to-day.

Can you tell the names of the four great winds? (East, West, North, South.)

Thursday

Have the children tell you about Æolus and his winds.

Friday

Write: The four winds are East, West, North and South.

THIRD WEEK

Monday

Talk about kites and kite-flying: How does a kite fly? How high will a kite fly? How do boys make kites?

Tell the children about the kites of Japan, and about kite-flying day in that country.

Tuesday

Have the children give as many words as they can that rhyme with *kite*. Write these on the blackboard, and use them for drill in phonics.

Wednesday

Talk about pussy willows. Who has seen pussy willows? Who has seen pussy willows this year? Where? How do we find the little pussies growing? What are they covered with? What for? (To protect the tiny buds from cold.)

Thursday

Write: Pussy willows have gray fur.

Friday

To be committed to memory:

Whatever way the wind doth blow,
Some heart is glad to have it so;
So blow it east, or blow it west,
The wind that blows—that wind is best.

FOURTH WEEK

Monday

Tell the children about St. Patrick, the good old Irish saint, whose birthday comes in March.

Tuesday

Have the children tell you about St. Patrick.

Wednesday

Write: *Spring begins in March.*

Thursday

Fill the blank spaces in the following:

The East Wind comes from the ——.
The West Wind comes from the ——.
The North Wind comes from the ——.
The South Wind comes from the ——.

Friday

Talk about the signs of Spring.

SECOND YEAR

FIRST WEEK

Monday

To be committed to memory:

THE WIND

I saw you toss the kites on high,
And blow the birds about the sky,
And all around I heard you pass,
Like ladies' skirts across the grass—
O wind, a-blowing all day long,
O wind, that sings so loud a song!

I saw the different things you did,
But always you yourself you hid.
I felt you push, I heard you call,
I could not see yourself at all—
O wind, a-blowing all day long,
O wind, that sings so loud a song!

O you that are so strong and cold;
O blower, are you young or old?
Are you a beast of field and tree,
Or just a stronger child than me?
O wind, a-blowing all day long?
O wind, that sings so loud a song?
—*Robert Louis Stevenson*

Children copy the first stanza of the poem, and commit it to memory.

Tuesday

Copy and learn the second stanza of the poem.

Wednesday

Copy and learn the third stanza of the poem.

Thursday

Recite the entire poem.

Friday

Write a list of the naming words (nouns) in the poem.

SECOND WEEK

Monday

For dictation:

Galloping, galloping, galloping in,
Into the world with a stir, and a din.
The north wind, the east wind, the west wind together,
In-bringing, in-bringing, the March's wild weather.

Tuesday

Write five sentences, telling what the wind does.

Wednesday

Story for reproduction:

SPRING

It was spring.

The sun had melted the snow from the hill-tops; the grass blades were pushing their way through the brown earth, and the buds on the trees were beginning to break open and let the tiny green leaves peep out.

A bee, waked from the sleep in which he had lain all through the winter, rubbed his eyes, then opened the door, and looked out to see if the ice and snow and the north wind had gone away. Yes; there was warm, clear sunshine.

He slipped out of the hive, stretched his wings and flew away.

He went to the apple tree and asked, "Have you anything for a hungry bee, who has eaten nothing the whole winter long?"

The apple tree answered:

"No; you have come too early. My blossoms are still buds and so I have nothing for you. Go to the cherry tree."

He flew to the cherry tree and said, "Dear cherry tree, have you any honey for a hungry bee?"

The cherry tree answered:

"Come again to-morrow; to-day my blossoms are shut up, but when they are open you are welcome to them."

Then he flew to a bed of tulips nearby. They had large, beautiful flowers, but there was neither sweetness nor perfume in them and he could not find any honey.

Tired and hungry, the poor bee turned to seek his home, when a tiny dark blue flower, beside a hedge, caught his eye.

It was a violet that was all ready for the bee's coming. The violet opened its cup of sweetness. The bee drank his fill, and carried some honey to the hive.

—Selected and Adapted

Thursday

Children retell, in their own words, the story of "Spring."

Friday

Write five sentences about spring.

THIRD WEEK

Monday

For dictation:

If a task is once begun,
Never leave it till it's done;
Be the labor great or small
Do it well, or not at all.

Tuesday

Talk about signs of spring! Sky, bright sun, warmer days, return of birds, pussy willows, swelling buds.

Wednesday

Write five sentences about pussy willows.

Thursday

Write a letter to your sister or brother, telling about pussy willow.

Friday

Write a sentence containing the word *blue*; one with the word *green*; *pink*; *yellow*; *red*; *white*.

FOURTH WEEK

Monday

Tell the children about St. Patrick.

Tuesday

Write three sentences about St. Patrick.

Wednesday

Write the names of all the members of the family, and your address.

Thursday

For dictation:

> Under the snowdrifts the blossoms are sleeping,
> Dreaming their dreams of sunshine and June.

Friday

Talk about the wind, and what it does.

THIRD YEAR

FIRST WEEK

Monday

To be committed to memory:

THE VOICE OF THE GRASS

Here I come creeping, creeping, everywhere;
By the dusty roadside,
On the sunny hillside,
Close by the noisy brook,
In every shady nook,
I come creeping, creeping everywhere.

Here I come creeping, creeping everywhere.
All around the open door,
Where sit the aged poor;
Here where the children play,
In the bright and merry May,
I come creeping, creeping everywhere.

Here I come creeping, creeping everywhere;
In the noisy city street
My pleasant face you'll meet,
Cheering the sick at heart.
Toiling his busy part—
Silently creeping, creeping everywhere.

Here I come creeping, creeping everywhere,
You cannot see me coming,
Nor hear my low sweet humming,
For in the starry night,

And the glad morning light,
I come quietly creeping, creeping everywhere.

Here I come creeping, creeping everywhere,
More welcome than the flowers
In summer's pleasant hours;
The gentle cow is glad,
And the merry bird not sad,
To see me creeping, creeping everywhere.

Here I come creeping, creeping everywhere;
My humble song of praise
Most joyfully I raise
To Him at whose command
I beautify the land,
Creeping, silently creeping everywhere.
—*Sarah Roberts Boyle*

Copy the first half of the poem.

Tuesday

Copy the rest of the poem.

Wednesday

Commit to memory the first two stanzas of the poem.

Thursday

Commit to memory the second two stanzas of the poem.

Friday

Recite the entire poem.

SECOND WEEK

Monday

Write a list of the nouns in the poem.

Tuesday

Write a list of the verbs in the poem.

Wednesday

Write a list of adjectives in the poem.

Thursday

For dictation:

In her dress of silver gray,
Comes the Pussy Willow gay;
Like a little Eskimo,
Clad in fur from top to toe.

Friday

Write five sentences about pussy willows.

THIRD WEEK

Monday

Write, to a classmate, a telegram of not more than ten words, saying that spring is coming.

Tuesday

Write a letter to a pussy willow.

Wednesday

Talk about the wind and what it does.

Thursday

Write five sentences telling what the wind does.

Friday

Write the story of St. Patrick.

FOURTH WEEK

Monday

For dictation:

> Day after day, and year after year,
> Little by little, the leaves appear;
> And the slender branches far and wide,
> Tell the mighty oak is the forest's pride.

Tuesday

Write a list of at least ten objects beginning with *m*. Who can write the longest list?

Wednesday

Write a rhyme of four lines about the wind.

Thursday

Write a story about some pet that you have or that you know about.

Friday

Tell something that makes you happy.

Tell something that makes you sorry.

Tell something that you think it is right to do.

Tell something that you think it is wrong to do.

FOURTH YEAR

FIRST WEEK

Monday

To be committed to memory:

THE FAIRIES

Up the airy mountain,
   Down the rushy glen,
We daren't go a-hunting,
   For fear of little men;
Wee folk, good folk,
   Trooping all together;
Green jacket, red cap,
   And white owl's feather.

Down along the rocky shore,
   Some make their home;
They live on crispy pancakes
   Of yellow tide-foam;
Some in the reeds
   Of the black mountain lake,

With frogs for their watch-dogs,
   All night awake.

High on the hilltop,
   The old king sits;
He is now so old and gray
   He's nigh lost his wits.
By the craggy hillside,
   Through the mosses bare,
They have planted thorn trees
   For pleasure here and there.
Is any man so daring,
   As dig one up in spite?
He shall find their sharpest thorns
   In his bed at night.

Up the airy mountain,
   Down the rushy glen,
We daren't go a-hunting,
   For fear of little men,
Wee folk, good folk,
   Trooping all together;
Green jacket, red cap;
   And white owl's feather.

—*William Allingham*

Copy the poem.

Tuesday

Learn the first half of the poem.

Wednesday

Learn the rest of the poem.

Thursday

Answer the following questions:

What is meant by the "airy" mountain?
What is meant by the "rushy glen"? What is a glen?
Why are the fairies called "wee" folk?
What is meant by their "trooping"?
What are "crispy" pan-cakes?
What are "reeds"?
Why is a mountain lake called "black"?

Friday

What "old king sits"?
What are "wits"?
What is a "craggy hillside"?
Why are the, mosses called "bare"?
Write a description of a fairy as given in the poem.

SECOND WEEK

Monday

Talk about the following: What story, that you have read, do you like best? Why? What game do you like best? Why? What song do you like best? Why? What study do you like best? Why?

Tuesday

For dictation:

Lives of great men all remind us,
 We can make our lives sublime;
And, departing, leave behind us,
 Footprints on the sands of time.

Wednesday

Write about what the wind does.

Thursday

Write about the signs of spring that you have noticed.

Friday

Talk about what you saw on your way to school.

THIRD WEEK

Monday

Write a list of all the words you can think of that begin with *h*. Who can write the longest list?

Tuesday

For dictation:

In spring when stirs the wind, I know
That soon the crocus buds will blow;
For 'tis the wind who bids them wake
And into pretty blossoms break.

Wednesday

Write a description of the teacher's desk.

Thursday

Write an informal invitation to a St. Patrick's Day entertainment at the school.

Friday

Have a spelling match.

FOURTH WEEK

Monday

Write seven verbs.

Write each in a different sentence.

Tuesday

For dictation:

To look up and not down,
To look forward and not back,
To look out and not in, and
To lend a hand.

Wednesday

Write a letter, if you are in the country, to some one in the city, telling what games you play at recess. If you live in the city, write to some one in the country.

Thursday

Write a description of some game you play.

Friday

Talk about the return of the birds.

APRIL

FIRST YEAR

FIRST WEEK

Monday

Talk about the next month? What is the name of this month? What was last month? What will next month be? What season is this? What will the next season be? How many days in April? What other months have only thirty days?

Tuesday

Story to be told to the children:

THE MORNING-GLORY SEED

A little girl dropped a morning-glory seed into a small hole in the ground. As she did so she said, "Now, morning-glory seed, hurry and grow, grow, grow, until you are a tall vine, covered with pretty green leaves and lovely trumpet flowers."

But the earth was very dry. There had been no rain for a long time, and the poor seed could not grow at all.

After it had lain in the ground for nine long days and nine long nights, the little seed said to the ground, "Oh, ground, please give me a few drops of water to soften my hard brown coat. Then my coat can burst open and set free my two green seed-leaves, and then I can begin to be a vine."

But the ground said, "You must ask that of the rain."

So the seed called to the rain. "Oh, rain," it said, "please come down and wet the ground around me, so that it may give me a few drops of water, to soften my hard brown coat. Then my coat can burst open and set free my two green seed-leaves, and then I can begin to be a vine."

"I cannot," said the rain, "unless the clouds hang low."

So the seed said to the clouds, "Oh, clouds, please hang low, and let the rain come down and wet the ground around me, so that it may give me a few drops of water to soften my hard brown coat. Then my coat can burst open and set free my two green seed-leaves, and then I can begin to be a vine."

But the clouds said, "The sun must hide first."

So the seed called to the sun. "Oh, sun, please hide for a little while. Then the clouds can hang low, and let the rain come down and wet the ground around me, so that it may give me a few drops of water, to soften my hard brown coat. Then my coat can burst open and set free my two green seed-leaves, and then I can begin to be a vine."

"I will," said the sun, and he hid at once.

Then the clouds hung low and lower. The rain began to fall fast and faster. The ground began to grow wet and wetter. The seed-coat began to grow soft and softer, until it burst open. Out came two bright green seed-leaves, and the morning-glory seed began to be a vine.—*Adapted*

Wednesday

Talk about the story of the morning-glory seed.

Thursday

Talk about the part the rain and the sunshine have in making plants grow.

Friday

Play as a game the story of the morning-glory seed.

SECOND WEEK

Monday

To be committed to memory:

SEVEN TIMES ONE

There's no dew left on the daisies and clover,
  There's no rain left in heaven;
I've said my "seven times" over and over,
  Seven times one are seven.

I am old, so old I can write a letter;
  My birthday lessons are done;
The lambs play always, they know no better,
  They are only one times one.

O moon! in the night I have seen you sailing,
  And shining so round and low;
You were bright, ah, bright! but your light is failing—
  You are nothing now but a bow.

You moon, have you done something wrong in heaven
  That God has hidden your face?
I hope if you have, you will soon be forgiven,
  And shine again in your place.

O velvet bee, you're a dusty fellow;
  You've powdered your legs with gold!
O brave marshmary buds, rich and yellow,
  Give me your money to hold.

And show me your nest with the young ones in it—
  I will not steal it away;
I am old! you may trust me, linnet, linnet—
  I am seven years old to-day!—*Jean Ingelow*

Spend the rest of the week teaching the poem to the children. They always enjoy this poem, one generation of little folks after another. Did you not?

THIRD WEEK

Monday

Talk about the rain: Why we need so much of it this month, when the plants are just starting to grow.

Tuesday

Have the children write: April is the rainy month.

Wednesday

For dictation:

> Oh, where do you come from,
> You little drops of rain?

Thursday

Read or recite the following poem to the children. Talk about where the rain comes from, and what becomes of the water. The children are old enough to understand and appreciate it all, if the explanation be made sufficiently simple.

THE RAIN DROPS' RIDE

Some little drops of water,
   Whose home was in the sea,
To go upon a journey
   Once happened to agree.

A white cloud was their carriage;
   Their horse, a playful breeze;
And over town and country
   They rode along at ease.

But, O! there were so many,
   At last the carriage broke,
And to the ground came tumbling
   Those frightened little folk.

Among the grass and flowers
   They then were forced to roam,
Until a brooklet found them,
   And carried them all home.—*Selected*

Friday

Let the children play the rain as a game. They can come from one part of the room which may represent the sea. They can ride on a play cloud. Coming gently to a garden, on the floor, they may play scatter the drops quietly, like an April rain, from their finger tips. Then they may join the brook, and go with it to where it enters the river, then follow the river to the ocean once more.

FOURTH WEEK

Monday

Tell the children the story of Paul Revere's Ride.

Tuesday

Have the children tell back to you the story of Paul Revere's Ride.

Wednesday

Read to the children Longfellow's poem, "Paul Revere's Ride."

Thursday

Write three sentences about Paul Revere's Ride.

Friday

Have the children play Paul Revere's Ride as a game.

SECOND YEAR

FIRST WEEK

Monday

A rainy morning. (If the morning is pleasant, use this exercise the first rainy day.) Why did you come to school this morning with rubbers and umbrella? Why does the rain run off an umbrella? Why is the roof of a house built on a slant? Why does rain sometimes fall straight down, and sometimes fall slanting? How does the rain tell us which way the wind blows? Why do rubbers keep our feet dry? Why do not our shoes keep our feet dry? What can you think of, besides overshoes, that is made of rubber?

Tuesday

Write five sentences about rain.

Wednesday

Poem to be committed to memory:

THE BLUEBIRD

I know the song the bluebird is singing,
Out in the apple tree where he is swinging,
Brave little fellow! the skies may be dreary—
Nothing cares he while his heart is so cheery.
Hark! how the music leaps from his throat!
Hark! was there ever so merry a note?

Listen a while, and you'll hear what he's saying,
Up in the apple tree swinging and swaying.
Dear little blossoms, down under the snow,
You must be weary of winter, I know;
Hark while I sing you a message of cheer:
Summer is coming, and springtime is here.

"Little white snowdrop, I pray you arise!
Bright yellow crocus, come open your eyes!
Sweet little violets, hid from the cold,
Put on your mantles of purple and gold!
Daffodils, daffodils! say, do you hear?
Summer is coming, and springtime is here.

—*Selected*

Have the poem copied.

Thursday

Learn the first and second stanzas of the poem.

Friday

Learn the rest of the poem.

SECOND WEEK

Monday

Write a list of the name words (nouns) in the poem, "The Bluebird."

Tuesday

Write a list of the doing words (verbs) in the poem.

Wednesday

Show the children a book. Show that damage done to a book will remain. If you scratch your finger, the wound heals. If you scratch a book, what happens? Do not break the back of the book. Never mark a book with pencil and ink. Especially never write anything in a book not your own. Do not turn down the corners of the leaves. Always return a borrowed book. Show the children how to open a new book properly.

Thursday

For dictation:

Little bird upon the bough,
Sing a song of sweetness now;
Sing of roses in their bloom,
In the lovely month of June,
Little bird upon the bough.

Friday

Read the following poem to the children. Talk about the woodpecker, and how he gets his food.

HOW THE WOODPECKER KNOWS

How does he know where to dig his hole,
The woodpecker there, on the elm-tree bole?
How does he know what kind of a limb
To use for a drum or burrow in?
How does he find where the young grubs grow?
I'd like to know!

The woodpecker flew to a maple limb,
And drummed a tattoo that was fun for him;
"No breakfast here! it's too hard for that!"
He said, as down on his tail he sat;
"Just listen to this, Rrrr-rat-tat-tat."—*Selected*

THIRD WEEK

Monday

Play "Animals": Give to each child a card having on it the name of some animal, as cat, horse, pig, etc. Have the children in turn describe the animals they represent as:

I am covered with hair. I gnaw bones. I watch at night to see that no one gets into the house. I say, "Bow, wow, wow," when I am happy. What am I?

Tuesday

For dictation:

He who plants a tree,
Plants a hope.

Wednesday

Talk about Arbor Day and Bird Day, and why we celebrate these special days. Why do they come in April rather than in January, or some other month?

Thursday

Write a list of all the trees you know about. Who can write the longest list?

Friday

Write a list of all the birds you know about. Who can write the longest list?

FOURTH WEEK

Monday

Tell the children the story of Paul Revere's Ride.

Tuesday

Have the children tell the story of Paul Revere's Ride.

Wednesday

Write five sentences about Paul Revere's Ride.

Thursday

Talk about the new parcel post. How are parcels sent? How heavy can parcels be sent? What can be sent by parcel post? How are letters sent? What does it cost to send a letter? A post card? How is the mail carried from place to place? How is the mail delivered in your town?

Friday

Write five sentences about the mails, and sending letters and parcels.

THIRD YEAR

FIRST WEEK

Monday

Write a list of objects you can see from a school-room window.

Tuesday

Write as many "signs of Spring," as you can think of.

Wednesday

For dictation:

All that's great and good is done
Just by patient trying.

Thursday

Read the following poem to the children:

WILD FLOWERS

Out amid the green fields,
  Free as air we grow,
Springing where it happens,
  Never in a row;
Watered by the cloudlets
  Passing overhead,
Warmed by lovely sunbeams,
  Falling on our heads.
Wild flowers, wild flowers, by the meadow rills,
Wild flowers, wild flowers, on the woody hills,
Wild flowers, wild flowers, springing everywhere,
  Joyful in the glad free air.—*Selected*

Talk about the coming of the wild flowers. What part have the rain and the sunshine in helping the flowers to grow? What wild flowers are in blossom now? What other flowers will blossom before the close of April?

Friday

Write eight sentences about wild flowers.

SECOND WEEK

Monday

Poem to be committed to memory: “The Owl and the Pussy Cat,” by Edward Lear.

Have the first half of the poem copied.

Tuesday

Have the rest of the poem copied.

Wednesday

Learn the first three stanzas of the poem.

Thursday

Learn the rest of the poem.

Friday

Allow the children to dramatize in their own way, "The Owl and the Pussy-cat."

THIRD WEEK

Monday

Write a list of the adjectives in "The Owl and the Pussycat."

Tuesday

Answer in complete sentences, the following questions:

What is the color of your reader? What is the color of your pencil? What is the color of your hair?

Wednesday

Write a rhyme of four lines about a cat.

Thursday

Have the children read "Paul Revere's Ride."

Friday

Have the children tell you the story of "Paul Revere's Ride."

FOURTH WEEK

Monday

Poem to be committed to memory:

WHAT DO WE PLANT?

What do we plant when we plant the tree?
We plant the ship, which will cross the sea,
We plant the mast to carry the sails;
We plant the plank to withstand the gales,
The keel, the keelson, and beam, and knee;
We plant the ship when we plant the tree.

What do we plant when we plant the tree?
We plant the houses for you and me;
We plant the rafters, the shingles, the floors;
We plant the studding, the lath, the doors,
The beams and siding, all parts that be;
We plant the house when we plant the tree.

What do we plant, when we plant the tree?
A thousand things that we daily see;
We plant the spire, that out-towers the crag;
We plant the staff for our country's flag;
We plant the shade, from the hot sun free—
We plant all these, when we plant the tree.

—*Henry Abbey*

Copy the poem.

Tuesday

Learn the first two stanzas of the poem.

Wednesday

Recite the entire poem.

Thursday

Write a list of the things we plant when we plant a tree.

Friday

Talk about the purpose of Arbor Day, and especially about the meaning of the beautiful Arbor Day poem.

FOURTH YEAR

FIRST WEEK

Monday

Story for reproduction:

THE CAT AND THE CHESTNUTS

A cat sat before an open fire where some chestnuts were roasting.

A monkey who was hungrily watching the chestnuts said to the cat, "Do you think you could pull a chestnut out of the fire? Your paws seem to be made just for that."

The cat was flattered and she quickly pulled out a chestnut that had burst open.

"How do you do it?" asked the monkey. "It is wonderful. Can you reach that big one?"

"Yes, but see, I have burned my paw a little."

"Oh, but what of that, when you are making yourself so useful?"

One after another the cat pulled the chestnuts from the fire. Then she found that the sly monkey had eaten them all. All she had was a pair of sore claws.

—*Æsop*

Tuesday

Write the story of the cat and the chestnuts.

Wednesday

Write ten sentences about the signs of spring.

Thursday

Write a list of the wild flowers that grow in your vicinity, so far as you know them.

Friday

Have each pupil draw on paper some kind of flower. Exchange papers, and each pupil write five sentences about the flower he thinks is intended by the drawing on the paper he receives.

SECOND WEEK

Monday

Poem to be committed to memory:

PLANT A TREE

He who plants a tree
Plants a hope.
Rootlets up through fibres blindly grope;
Leaves unfold into horizons free.
So man's life must climb
From the clods of time
Unto heavens sublime.
Can'st thou prophesy, thou little tree,
What the glory of thy boughs shall be?

He who plants a tree
Plants a joy.
Plants a comfort that will never cloy.
Everyday a fresh reality,
Beautiful and strong,
To whose shelter throng
Creatures blithe with song.

If thou could'st but know, thou happy tree,
Of the bliss that shall inhabit thee!

He who plants a tree
He plants peace.
Under its green curtains jargons cease;
Leaf and zephyr murmur soothingly;
Shadows soft with sleep
Down tired eyelids creep,
Balm of slumber deep.
Never hast thou dreamed, thou blessed tree,
Of the benediction thou shalt be.

He who plants a tree
He plants youth;
Vigor won for centuries, in sooth;
Life of time, that hints eternity!
Boughs their strength uprear,
New shoots every year
On old growths appear.
Thou shalt teach the ages, sturdy tree,
Youth of soul is immortality.

He who plants a tree
He plants love;
Tents of coolness spreading out above
Wayfarers he may not live to see.
Gifts that grow are best;
Hands that bless are blest;
Plant: life does the rest!
Heaven and earth help him who plants a tree,
And his work its own reward shall be.—*Lucy Larcom*

Copy the poem.

Tuesday

Learn the first two stanzas of the poem.

Wednesday

Learn the second two stanzas of the poem.

Thursday

Learn the rest of the poem.

Friday

Talk about the meaning of the hope, joy, peace, youth, and love, as mentioned in the poem.

THIRD WEEK

Monday

Write a list of twenty articles made of wood.

Tuesday

Each pupil think of a tree. Each in turn tell about his tree, the other pupils to guess what it is. For instance:

I am tall and straight. I have many long needles, instead of leaves. When the wind blows through my branches it makes sweet music. What am I? (A pine tree.)

Or—I am a large tree, with great branches. My fruit is called an acorn. What am I? (An oak tree.)

Wednesday

Talk about Arbor Day—why it is celebrated, and why it is necessary that our trees be preserved.

Thursday

For dictation:

A song to the oak! the brave old oak!
  Who hath ruled in the greenwood long;
Here's health and renown to his broad green crown
  And his fifty arms so strong.

FOURTH WEEK

Monday

Story for reproduction:

TRIFLES

A friend of the great artist, Michael Angelo, was once watching the last touches being made to a statue. Some time later he visited the studio again, and the artist was still at work upon the same statue. He exclaimed: "You have done nothing since the last time I was here. The statue was finished then."

"Not at all," was Michael Angelo's reply. "I have softened this feature and brought out that muscle. I have given more expression to the lips and more energy to the eye."

"Oh," said the friend, "but these are trifles."

"It may be so," said the artist, "but trifles make perfection and perfection is no trifle."

Tuesday

Write ten sentences, each containing *is* or *are*.

Wednesday

Write sentences, each of which contains one of the following adjectives; little, yellow, moist, good, large, beautiful, swift, slow, useful, breakable.

Thursday

For dictation:

> Tinkling down! shining down!
>   Golden sunbeams kiss the flowers.
> Wake them up! wake them up!
>   Through the happy hours.

Friday

Play "What I am thinking of," using objects in the school-room.

MAY

FIRST YEAR

FIRST WEEK

Monday

What is the name of this month? What is the name of the month just ended? What is the name of the month following May? What season is this? What season follows spring? How many days has May? What other months have thirty-one days?

Tuesday

Teach the proper method of salutation on the street. Have the boys put on their caps, and the girls their hats. Have a boy and a girl go to the front of the room, and from opposite sides of the room walk toward each other. As they meet, the girl nods her head politely, and the boy lifts his hat. After the simple ceremony the two children return to their seats, and their places are taken by other boys and girls, in turn, until all can make the proper salutation easily and gracefully.

Wednesday

Write a sentence about birds.

Write a sentence about the grass.

Write a sentence about May.

Thursday

Story for reproduction. (Let the children test the results of mixing colors, with their paint boxes, if they have paints.)

THE RAINBOW FAIRIES

One night three little fairies were playing under a tree. They were flower fairies. Each had on a dress of the same color as the flower for which it was named. Little Fairy Buttercup wore a bright yellow dress. Forget-me-not wore a blue dress. Geranium wore a red dress.

Not far from the three fairies in red, yellow and blue, were three other fairies. These fairies had on old, faded dresses. They stood and watched the gaily-dressed fairies dance in the moonlight.

"Come," said Buttercup, "won't you come and dance with us?"

"We cannot," said the three. "We cannot dance, for we have on our old clothes. We have worked hard all day and are just going home, but we like to see you dance in your pretty clothes."

Then Buttercup took the skirt of her yellow dress and dipped it into a lily cup filled with dew. The dew was quickly dyed yellow.

Forget-me-not dipped the skirt of her blue dress into another lily cup filled with dew. The dew was quickly dyed blue. Then the fairies mixed the yellow dew and the blue dew together.

"Now jump in, little fairy," cried Buttercup. In jumped one of the fairies in faded gown, and when she came out her dress was a beautiful green.

Then Geranium dipped her dress into dew, and Forget-me-not did the same. They mixed blue and red, and the second fairy jumped in. When she came out, her dress was bright purple.

Then Buttercup and Geranium dipped their dresses into dew again, to make a mixture for the third fairy. When she came out of the lily cup her dress was bright orange.

Then the six fairies laughed and sang, and danced about. By and by a dark cloud covered the moon, and the rain came pattering down. The six fairies hid themselves in the flowers.

The next morning, when the rain stopped, the sun came out and shone brightly. The six fairies came out of the flowers, and hand in hand they ran up to the sky. There they made a beautiful rainbow. Since then, they have been called the Rainbow Fairies.—*Adapted*

Friday

Talk about the rainbow, and its six colors. Have the children tell the combinations that make green, purple, and orange.

SECOND WEEK

Monday

To be committed to memory:

THE DANDELION

A brave little dandelion woke up from his nap,
And hunted around in the dark for his cap,
"I'm certain," he muttered, "it ought to be here,
In the very same place where I left it last year."

He poked all about in the dirt and the dark,
For the same little hat that he wore in the ark;
For fashions may vary with people and clime,
But dandelions wear the same hats all the time.

"What's o'clock?" and he paused while he counted the fuzz
That had crept through his locks, as old age always does;
Then he settled himself to pluck out the old feathers,
That had done so much service in all kinds of weathers.

Rather frowsy he looked, getting into his hat,
But he knew that the rain would take care of all that,
If he only were up; so he pulled on his boots,
And began to push up from his tough little roots.

Kept pushing, and cheerful and hopeful, he pushed,
And he came to the surface, close by an old bush,
With the frost hardly gone, and the ground hardly mellow,
Here he is on the top now, the brave little fellow.

The first dandelion! Well may we delight
And call all the children to see the glad sight,
For of all the brave prospects of hope and of spring,
The golden-crowned dandelion surely is king.

—Selected and slightly adapted

Teach the children the first stanza of the poem.

Tuesday

Teach the children the second stanza of the poem.

Wednesday

Teach the children the third stanza of the poem, explaining what is meant by the "fuzz."

Thursday

Teach the fourth stanza of the poem.

Friday

Teach the fifth stanza of the poem.

THIRD WEEK

Monday

Teach the sixth stanza of the poem.

Tuesday

Have the children play the poem, each child acting the part of the dandelion, as all recite the poem in concert.

Wednesday

Write:

A dandelion is yellow.
Dandelions bloom in May.

Thursday

Children name a flower (besides dandelions) that is yellow; one that is blue; green; pink; white; purple. Which of these are in blossom in May?

Friday

Talk about different kinds of dogs, and what each is good for; *e. g.*, terrier, catching rats; collie, driving sheep; St. Bernard, saving life; hound, hunting, etc.

FOURTH WEEK

Monday

What flowers bloom in May? What are their colors? What are the birds doing this month? Have you seen any birds' nests this spring? Where? What kinds of birds do you know? What have the trees been doing this month? (Growing leaves.)

Tuesday

Ask each child to bring a penny to school.

See how many things can be found on the penny.

What is the motto of our country? (In God we trust.)

Wednesday

Have the children write:

Under the green trees,
  Just over the way,
Jack-in-the-pulpit
  Preaches to-day.

Thursday

Have the pupils told, the preceding day, to bring into the school-room three different green objects, as a leaf from a tree, a blade of grass, a branch of some plant, etc. Have pupils write the words describing what they have brought, as leaf, grass, twig, etc.

Friday

Talk about Decoration Day. What it means, and how to celebrate it.

SECOND YEAR

FIRST WEEK

Monday

Learn the first two stanzas of the poem:

THE SEED

As wonderful things are hidden away
   In the heart of a little brown seed
As ever were found in the fairy nut
   Of which we sometimes read.

Over the dainty shining coat,
   We sprinkle the earth so brown,
And then the sunshine warms its bed,
   And the rain comes pattering down.

Patter, patter, the soft warm rain
   Knocks at the tiny door,
And two little heads come peeping out,
   Like a story in fairy lore.
      —*Selected and slightly adapted*

Tuesday

Learn the entire poem.

Wednesday

Talk about the meaning of the poem, and sow some morning glory seed in a box or flower pot. Talk about the need of moist earth to make the seeds grow. Have the children water the seeds every day, until the “two little heads come peeping out.”

Thursday

Write a list of the naming words (nouns) in the poem of the week.

Friday

Children write five sentences about seeds and the way they grow.

SECOND WEEK

Monday

For dictation:

Sing, O sing, thou merry bird,
As you fly so lightly;
Sing your song of joy and love,
While the sun shines brightly.

Tuesday

Write, in complete sentences, answers to the following questions:

What bird has a red breast? (Robin.)

What bird picks worms from under the bark of large trees? (Woodpecker.)

What bird lays large white eggs that we like to eat for breakfast? (Hen.)

What bird likes to eat the farmer's corn? (Crow.)

What bird says, "Coo, coo, coo?" (Pigeon.)

Wednesday

Talk about the birds and nest-building. Talk about the different kinds of nests: the robin's; the oriole's, hung from the limb of a tall tree; the bobolink's, built in the grass; the sparrow's, tucked under the eaves; the swallow's, built in the barn, etc.

Thursday

Read the following poem to the children, and have them tell the story back to you:

THE JOLLY OLD CROW

On the limb of an oak sat a jolly old crow,
And chattered away with glee, with glee,
As he saw the old farmer go out to sow,
And he cried, "It's all for me, for me!

"Look, look, how he scatters his seeds around;
He's tremendously kind to the poor, the poor;
If he'd empty it down in a pile on the ground.
I could find it much better, I'm sure, I'm sure!

"I've learned all the tricks of this wonderful man,
Who shows such regard for the crow, the crow,
That he lays out his grounds on a regular plan,
And covers his corn in a row, a row!

"He must have a very great fancy for me;
He tries to entrap me enough, enough,
But I measure his distance as well as he,
And when he comes near I am off!"—*Selected*

Friday

Have the children write a little story about the crow and the corn.

THIRD WEEK

Monday

Write five words beginning with *m*.

Write five words beginning with *s*.

Write five words beginning with *b*.

Tuesday

Add a word to *violet,* to show what color it is.

Add a word to *tulip,* to show what color it is.

Add a word to *apple blossom,* to show what color it is.

Add a word to *hyacinth,* to show what color it is.

Add a word to *grass,* to show what color it is.

Wednesday

For dictation:

Into my window a sunbeam bright
Comes with a glad good morning,
"The night is gone, it is time you were up,"
It is thus he gives me warning.

Thursday

Write five sentences, telling what the warm sunshine does.

Friday

Play, as a game, "I went to the woods and brought back a violet." One child says, "I went to the woods, and brought back a violet and an anemone" (or any other flower). The next child says, "I went to the woods and brough back a violet, an anemone, and a hepatica." Each child adds a flower to the list, as long as the children can remember the list of flowers.

FOURTH WEEK

Monday

Talk about birds' eggs, and the wrong of robbing nests.

Tuesday

Read the following poem to the children:

THE FRIGHTENED BIRDS

"Hush! hush!" said the little brown thrush,
To her mate on the nest in the alder bush.
"Keep still! don't open your bill,
There's a boy coming bird-nesting over the hill.

"Let go your wings out, so
That not an egg on the nest shall show.
Chee! chee! it seems to me
I'm as frightened as ever a bird can be."

Then still, with a quivering bill,
They watched the boy out of sight o'er the hill.
And then, in the branches again
Their glad song rang out over valley and glen.

Oh! oh! if only that boy could know
How glad they were when they saw him go,
Say, do you think that next day,
He could possibly steal those eggs away?

—*Selected*

Talk about the advantage that the birds are, in eating insects and protecting the trees.

Wednesday

Write five sentences, telling what birds do for us, and why it is wrong to steal birds' eggs.

Thursday

Fill the blank spaces in the following:

—— blackbirds —— on a hill,
One named ——, the other —— Jill.
Fly away ——,
—— away, Jill,
Come ——, Jack,
—— back, ——.

Friday

Write a letter to your cousin, telling about birds, and why you will never steal their eggs.

THIRD YEAR

FIRST WEEK

Monday

Poem to be committed to memory:

WE THANK THEE

For flowers that bloom about our feet;
For tender grass, so fresh, so sweet;
For song of bird and hum of bee;
For all things fair we hear or see,
  Father in heaven, we thank Thee!

For blue of stream and blue of sky;
For pleasant shade of branches high;
For fragrant air and cooling breeze;
For beauty of the blooming trees—
  Father in heaven, we Thank Thee!

For mother-love and father-care,
For brothers strong and sisters fair;
For love at home and here each day;
For guidance, lest we go astray—
  Father in heaven, we Thank Thee!—*Selected*

Have the poem copied.

Tuesday

Learn the first stanza of the poem.

Wednesday

Learn the second stanza of the poem.

Thursday

Learn and recite the entire poem.

Friday

Write a list of the nouns in the poem.

SECOND WEEK

Monday

Write a list of the adjectives in the poem.

Tuesday

Write the name of a flower that is blue; one that is yellow; pink; red; purple; white. Write a sentence describing each of the flowers in your list.

Wednesday

Write the name of a bird that is brown; one that is black; blue; green; yellow. Class exchange papers. Write a sentence about each bird on the list you receive.

Thursday

Talk about May, and how it differs from any other month of the year. What garden flowers are in blossom this month? What wild flowers are in blossom? What fruit trees? What forest trees?

Friday

Write five sentences about the flowers and trees that blossom in May.

THIRD WEEK

Monday

Story for reproduction:

ANEMONE

Once upon a time there lived a youth whose name was Adonis. He was a fine-looking boy, tall and straight, and he was very fond of hunting.

Every day, with only his dogs for company, he would go into the woods, carrying his bow and arrows. He had a fast horse on which he rode.

His friends often urged him not to go too far into the deep woods, but Adonis was not at all afraid. He had killed bears, and he had killed lions, so why should he be afraid?

One day Adonis was in the woods as usual, when he caught sight of two wild hogs. He left his dogs to worry one of the hogs, and he started after the other with his spear.

The angry hog bit him and he had to hasten to the brook to bathe his wounds. The angry hog followed him.

Swimming in the brook were some beautiful white swans. When they saw Adonis wounded, they went to Venus and told her what they had seen.

Venus hastened to the brook in her silver chariot.

"Adonis! Adonis!" she cried.

No answer came. The only trace she could find of Adonis was some drops of blood on the green grass.

Venus was very sorry, for she loved the boy Adonis very much. From a silver cup which she carried with her, she sprinkled a few drops of blood over the grass. In a little while, tiny flower buds peeped out from the spot where each drop of blood had fallen.

A gentle wind came up and blew the little buds open and before night it had blown them all away. People called the little flowers wind-flowers, or anemones. Their delicate pink coloring was believed to have come from the heart of Adonis. Have you seen the dainty little anemones, the wind-flowers?
—*Adapted*

Tell the story to the children.

Tuesday

Have the children tell back to you the story of the anemones.

Wednesday

Write the story of the anemones.

Thursday

Write five sentences about the woods where the anemones grow.

Friday

Have the children play in their own way the story of Adonis.

Milton Keynes UK
Ingram Content Group UK Ltd.
UKHW051818050424
440683UK00011B/288

9 781805 476856